UNIV... ...INGHAM

WITHDRAWN

ROM THE LIBRAR

D0233100

K2

Each In His Office

EACH
IN HIS OFFICE

Studies of Men in Power

BY

GEORGE MALLABY

Leo Cooper . London

UNIVERSITY LIBRARY
NOTTINGHAM

First published in Great Britain, 1972 by
LEO COOPER LTD,
196 Shaftesbury Avenue, London WC2

Copyright © GEORGE MALLABY 1972

ISBN 0 85052 076 2   1002935872

Printed in Great Britain at
The Compton Press
Salisbury

T

Contents

This book is dedicated to the
memory of four very different but
very remarkable men who figure
prominently in its pages

Norman Brook
Henry Kendall
H W Garrod
Jack Adams

Foreword

There is in this age, it seems, a compelling desire in the hearts of many men for power and for opportunities to exercise it, and at the same time considerable mistrust—or is it envy?—of those who, in the common view, have this power and exercise it continuously. The interest in this power game has grown so strong in many countries that academic institutions have sprung up like mushrooms with the expressed intention of teaching men techniques which will enable them to exercise power over others and to make decisions, rapidly and expertly, which will affect the achievements of the organisation for which they work and consequently the lives and happiness of others who work in it. Decision-making has become a subject of intense general interest, demanding research and profound study. How are decisions made? How can they be made more rapidly and how can they be guaranteed to be a good deal more fool-proof than they are now? There are technological inventions which not only aid these enquiries but can also be turned to the assistance of those institutions where decisions, based on the fullest possible evidence, are daily essential. Nobody is likely to deny this. Great commanders in war, who, in the heat and fury of a modern battle, are obliged to make split-second decisions affecting the victory of their cause and the lives of their soldiers, would be grateful for any inventions or techniques which would ensure that they take these vital decisions on the fullest and most up-to-date information available. But they would still insist that they themselves, isolated and tortured human beings, must alone be responsible for the decisions taken. That is certainly true, and it is true of all those who have to take ultimate decisions, whatever the world in which they work, whether they are Prime Ministers, prominent public servants, fighting men, or, I suppose, gangsters and crooks. The success of an enterprise depends upon the decision taken at a critical moment of time. The importance of this crucial decision and the range and scope of its consequences will vary with the

7

importance of the enterprise. The Prime Minister, for example, may in theory take a decision, or lead his Government to a decision, which will plunge a whole nation into war or one which will suddenly impoverish a large part of it by penal taxation and by drastically curtailing the number of jobs on offer. It was to curb and check this excessive power in the hands of one man, or one small group of men, that a system of Parliamentary Democracy came gradually into being. Men were unwilling to give their docile obedience to a man who, because of the accident of his birth, claimed a divine right to govern and command his subjects as he thought fit. If no wiser humilities were likely to come out of his head, then he had better lose his head; and so he did. But there was still a long struggle and a rough progression through factious oligarchies towards a system of universal suffrage generally expected to curb the powers of the oligarchy, which was in the habit of taking far-reaching decisions behind closed doors and without much respect for the popular will, in so far as that could be ascertained. As the power of Parliament grew greater, the power of the Executive would grow less; or so it was expected. But now it is believed in many quarters that Parliament is nothing, that M.P.s may talk away—sometimes with wise eloquence, sometimes in incoherent folly—voting and abstaining, questioning and accusing, criticising, applauding, without deflecting by one hair's breadth the opinions and decisions of that handful of men, selected by the Prime Minister and led by him, known as the Cabinet and meeting regularly and in the utmost secrecy at No. 10 Downing Street.

The political theorists, the so-called Professors of Politics, can pursue that argument. What I have attempted to do in my first chapter is to see this problem in personal terms, to take a look at a selection of the leading political figures of my lifetime, some of whom I have been able to observe at first hand. I wanted to view them as human beings, to seek to understand their motives in entering politics at all, and to watch them exercising the power which they had achieved. Political philosophers can usefully concern themselves with learned argument in support of a general proposition that the Prime Minister and his Cabinet in this country enjoy too much power. I thought it interesting to see how individual Prime

Ministers in this century came to achieve that power, how they exercised it and whether in fact they did enjoy it. They are, after all, a very mixed bunch. There is no stereotype, no professional stigma, no uniform, no clipped moustache and short hair, no formal conventions of dress or undress. It would never occur to anyone to place in the same category or club, the humdrum Attlee and the flamboyant Lloyd George, or to attribute similar motives and qualities to the tranquillising Baldwin and the combative Churchill.

Any study of the power of politicians leads inevitably to questions about the power of their advisers; and indeed it is a matter of public comment and concern that those faceless anonymities, the senior civil servants, exercise substantial power over the Ministers they are supposed to serve. Angry and malevolent critics will complain that these men, in no sense representative of the popular will, impose, behind a cloak of official secrecy, their own fossilised and conventional opinions upon the elected representatives of the people. The procedures by which civil servants reach the advice they offer to Ministers should be openly seen, they demand. Even worse than televising the debates in Parliament would be the televising of Whitehall wranglings, the disputes, the discussions, the sifting of evidence, the questioning, the probing which precede the submission of advice to a Minister. It is true, nevertheless, that senior civil servants do exercise considerable power. Whether it is too much and whether it is in the hands of the right type of civil servant can be argued by academic pundits steeped in theoretical administration. I have contented myself with examining the personal attitudes and ambitions of civil servants I have known, of presenting them to my readers as human beings, of asking whether these men wanted power and how they exercised it. I spent a good many years amongst them, working with them, admiring their methods and their intellectual integrity, astonished by their tireless uncomplaining industry. They have their weaknesses like other men; but they are men, not just unseen official advisers, and it is as men that some of them walk through my pages. It is a part of their duty to avoid and disdain the limelight. They never looked for fame, but their absolute devotion to duty has fitted some of them to receive it.

9

In the same sort of category are the top fighting men, whom I discuss in my third chapter. In war-time they achieve a splendid, perhaps an undying fame. In peace-time they are comparatively unknown. Theorists may argue that in constitutional terms they have too much, or too little, power. Again I have seen them in human terms, in war-time as far as I knew them, and in peace as I viewed them in the conduct of everyday affairs. I grew up in the shadow of the First World War and escaped by less than two years being included in what many now think its senseless and useless sacrifice. In 1920, to those of us who were just coming to manhood, war seemed abhorrent and we were blindly, though perhaps excusably, determined to have nothing whatever to do with anything military. I remember the lengths of evasion and deception to which I went, when a freshman at Oxford in 1920, in order to escape being enrolled in the Senior O.T.C. We had had enough of drilling and marching and fighting mock battles, ordered hither and thither by rough command, subjected to a harsh discipline by jacks-in-office who loved to exercise their autocratic power. Besides we were idealists and Woodrow Wilson was our hero. I saw him arrive at Victoria Station one bright morning in December, 1918, and he seemed to my young eyes a prophet and a law-giver coming from the New World to give fresh life and hope to the Old. It was many years before I gave up my faith in the League of Nations and shared in the general disillusionment with Wilsonian idealism. In all those years I eschewed the military art and joined in the ignorant chorus of contempt and dislike for Colonel Blimp and those inflexible Generals who were thought to be only too anxious for another war. Inwardly I must have had reservations about this short-sighted silliness; and of course I excused my much-loved brother because he was in the Indian Army and their role was quite different. In time I came to see the absolute value of strong and highly professional fighting services for keeping the peace; and as my acquaintanceship with military men was extended, I found much gentleness of feeling and much compassion beneath the clipped decisive manner which turns every conversation into a lecture, and will not allow any doubt or speculation about national and international affairs. In military circles there are only a few war-mongers and the lovers of power are mostly in the lower ranks. What were the motives, I wondered, which induced young men to enter the fighting services and how did they exercise the power they undoubtedly had?

The more I related power to personality the more my thoughts turned to the creation of personality and the factors which contribute to its make-up. Heredity is an inescapable factor, perhaps more decisive than is sometimes thought, but the experience of all wise men would stoutly assert some freedom of will, some licence to rise above, or below, the genes which did so much dictating at their birth, and would repudiate as quite unacceptable a resigned surrender to any arid theory of predestination. Amongst the early influences in a man's life are the personalities of his parents, his brothers and sisters, the environment in which the family lives and the type of friends they have; and not the least influence is the influence of some schoolmasters. This influence can be very strong. Many men, I daresay, will hardly remember most of their schoolmasters at all, faint and ineffectual figures in a distant charade, but they will certainly remember their school; and the impression it made on them, for good or ill, is, to some extent at least, attributable to the Headmaster and the organisation and atmosphere he created around him. Others will cherish recollections of one or two particular men, who by precept and example opened their eyes to an expanding world of mental and physical activity and first induced in them a sense of spiritual and intellectual wonder. A good schoolmaster has notable power over sensitive and impressionable boys. It is not the same as the power of a Prime Minister. It does not alter the course of history, but it may alter in some subtle way the personality, the ambitions and the hopes of a young man. In a society like ours, embracing ideas of personal freedom and Christian insistence on the importance of the individual, this is a power, substantial, significant and to be exercised with the utmost care. In my fourth chapter I have examined the power of Headmasters and assistant masters in independent schools, the only type of school of which I have first-hand knowledge. The missionary zeal of the great Victorian Headmasters has given place to a less earnest attitude, but no less solicitous and dedicated, in the Headmasters of today. The opportunities for the exercise of power still persist. Do men enter the school-master's profession because they are anxious to achieve power over others and how do they use the opportunities to exercise it? That is my theme.

I have never been a university don (though I was for some years an Extraordinary Fellow of a Cambridge College), but I have always had many close contacts in that world from my undergraduate days onwards. Men with a taste for learning, however unlearned they themselves may be, and enough wit to indulge in rash and radical thinking, look upon dons with admiration and something like envy. They are so deeply versed, so splendidly professional, in their own subjects and so attractively clever and provocative about other people's. They can, and often do, have great influence on young men, teaching them to use their intellectual capacity to the full, filling their heads with knowledge and seducing them into strange ways of thought. An attachment to instruction and advice is not always the mark of a don and before 1820 or so was probably very rare. Dons at Oxford and Cambridge went their own idle way and undergraduates got on as well as they could. The distinguished alumni of whom Colleges now boast, had little respect or affection for their mentors. In the world of literature, University College, Oxford, sent Shelley down and only many years later tried to make amends by enshrining him in naked marble. At Cambridge, Coleridge ran away from Jesus and Wordsworth was by no means in love with St John's, and never established close personal relationships with any of his tutors. He was pleased enough, I daresay, that his portrait should take its place close to "Margaret, the saintly foundress", but he never felt that his renown owed anything to the influence of his College. Since his day the attitude of dons to undergraduates has changed. There is more interest, more solicitude, and I was indeed fortunate in the influences which played upon my young mind and heart when I went up to Merton in 1920. The debt is different in many respects from the debt men owe to their schoolmasters. The motives and ambitions of dons are quite distinct, but they cannot escape exercising considerable power, beneficial or not, over adolescent minds.

In no profession is everyone docile and obedient, always ready to toe the party line, always at hand with safe and

12

careful advice, always content with the school solution, unquestionably loyal in every particular to *The Lanchester Tradition*[1] and never rashly swerving away from disciplined and objective thinking. In all professions there are rebels and most professions would become very stagnant without them. Rebels have a lot of influence in the world, even though they may never achieve power and place. They are perpetual gadflies and by persistent stinging they win a point or two outright from time to time. Moreover, the powers-that-be, conscious of the obtrusive buzzing of these gadflies and anxious to forestall the sharp pain of a sting, introduce into their speeches and their legislation opinions and acts designed to conciliate and mollify. In politics James Maxton, never in office, was a notably successful rebel, eloquent, persuasive and humane; and he made his rebelliousness more effective by being convivial and popular with all men. Some rebels disdain friendship, preferring to sit sullen in a corner, only emerging to display yet one more chip on a capacious shoulder. These out-and-out rebels, who can never be tempted to turn game-keeper, are more frequently found in politics than in the other professions I have considered. The prickly non-conformist, the unrelenting anti-man, could not find a permanent place in any branch of the public service. There are such, but sooner or later they can stand it no longer. The required docility is beyond them. They resign and devote their energies to the propagation of their ideas by books and journalism. Sir Basil Liddell-Hart and Major General J. F. C. Fuller are notable examples. A dear friend of mine, Lieutenant-General Sir Frederick Morgan, just about stayed the course, but not without scenes and upsets, hostility and impatience amongst those to whom he was subordinate. He had a maxim in life, which he passed on to me, a piece of worldly wisdom, mixed with righteous principle—'Never resign. If you think you are right, stick to it. If all the same "they" sack you, "they" will probably feel obliged to give you some form of compensation.' I have never had the courage to act on this advice.

In the academic world there are many rebels. Every school common-room has more than one rebel, resolute to pour scorn

[1] *The Lanchester Tradition* by G. F. Bradby (1914).

on every decision made by the Headmaster, contemptuous of the organisation and the aims of the school which he is supposed to be serving, angry with conventional modes and manners. His voice is listened to at first, attention is paid to his reforming zeal; but if he continues isolated, disagreeable and ungenerous, never content, never ready for a wise compromise and fruitful reconciliation, his power and influence depart. If he does not depart also, he descends into a middle age of irritable and ineffective seclusion, boys and masters equally impatient for the day of his retirement. Schools—all kinds of schools—are in fact an integral part of the Establishment, and no schools more so than those which are called independent. Universities are very different and in that society the rebel has a happy lack of restraint. Indeed every university don, even the most conservative, could in one sense be called a trained iconoclast. All opinions, all beliefs, all standards, all so-called principles, all accepted knowledge must be brought to the bar and thoroughly probed and examined. No proposition can be accepted without supporting evidence, no instinctive feeling recognised and certainly no hunch admitted. The intellect is supreme. If this is the basis of university teaching there is much more to it than that, and very soon the intellect itself must be called in question. What is it and who made it? Where in a man does it reside and how does it operate? Only the Provost of King's is likely to give confident answers to those questions. For the rest, philosophers, physiologists, chemists, biologists, physicists, classicists, historians and linguists swim uncertainly in a sea of doubt, anxious not seldom to keep one toe upon the ground. Arts and sciences, in spite of formulation, classification and systematic analysis cannot uncover the innermost mysteries. Ultimately the intellectual arrogance of many dons admits interference from moral sensibilities and incommunicable feelings. But still the university is not, and never should be, a part of the Establishment and so long as it can retain its academic freedom (it has no other) it can accommodate in its libertarian embrace every sort of rebel, constructive and destructive, shallow and profound. For this reason there is in Chapter VI no university rebel. In that chapter I have illustrated the rebel personality for the most part by reference to men who have been induced to turn aside from their rebellion and serve the established order in some form. In politics Aneurin Bevan is a shining example and in the world of social problems, industrial difficulties and local politics I have chosen John Jackson Adams, later Lord Adams of Ennerdale, as the very human hero of my discourse.

The six categories of my inquisition are known to me at first hand. Though I was never a politician or a university don and my military experience was almost exclusively confined to Whitehall, I have moved near enough to these professions to be able to judge more or less what each in his office designs and desires, and wherever I have moved I have never been free from inner visitations of rebellious dissent. There are many other offices in which power resides and these I can view only as an outsider; I have taken a rather cursory look at some of them in my seventh chapter.

I reserve my last chapter for a discussion of the influence of women, an influence wider and more profound than some of them imagine but most powerfully exercised, not by design, but by instinctive love.

Chapter 1

THE POLITICIAN

No subject, except perhaps religion, is more able to stimulate heated, ill-informed and fruitless argument than politics. At every level of society the debate continues. In factory canteens, in public houses, in school common-rooms, in London clubs, in upper-middle-class drawing rooms, in the last inhabited corners of ducal palaces, men and women harangue each other on the issues of the day, taking sides upon questions which they do not understand, making free with accusations of bad faith and evil intentions, liberal with slander and personal abuse, without any sensation of unfair or illogical dealing, translating the merits and demerits of some kind of rent act into a violent attack upon the Prime Minister's private life, attributing tribal warfare in the deserts of Arabia to the eccentric personal habits of the Foreign Secretary—always at the end of the argument talking in terms of personalities, not plans, of men and not measures. For many years I was happy to break a lance in this absurd fray and to advance ill-founded views with arrogant conviction. Now I am only too ready to withdraw my attention and think about Tom Thumb, more particularly in that kind of society in which the insolent assumption is made that all are of the same opinion and inflexibly attached to the same cause. 'Do you think we shall get them out next time?' is a question often put to me in respectable county homes and even a natural inclination to the politeness of silence cannot prevent me from enquiring roughly who 'we' are and what is meant by 'they'. Thus confronted, the questioner inevitably has recourse to, 'But surely you don't like the present occupant of No. 10!' 'Like' —how should one like or dislike a man one has hardly seen except on television and never spoken to? And what relevance does this liking or disliking have to the virtue of his policies? It is the personalities, it seems, which rouse the passions of many of the electors. My grandfather, I was told, seemed at times unalterably convinced that Gladstone was the creation of Satan. I was not old enough to ask him to defend this extreme position before he himself was called away to join Gladstone in an everlasting political limbo. When I first went to Washington in 1944, when the tide had triumphantly turned and victory was within the grasp of American and British arms, when the energies and efforts of Roosevelt and Churchill were about to be crowned, I was astonished to be asked by the woman sitting next to me at dinner, 'Well! What do you think of the lunatic in the White House?' I had not realised until that moment how deeply and sharply Roosevelt's personality had divided his country, in spite of the single over-riding national aim of defeating the enemy. A few months later it seemed an inexcusable lack of gratitude and a strange deviation of taste on the part of the British electorate to prefer Attlee to Churchill. But there were more fundamental reasons for this peculiarity of choice, and indeed the General Election of 1945 is certainly one of which it can be emphatically stated that personality was not the deciding factor. Winston had won the war. By his unrelenting vigour, his energy of hatred and contempt for an evil man, his persistent initiative, his individual eloquence, with its mixture of majestic phrases, pungent brevities and characteristically English humour, and by his indomitable pugnacity he had saved his country from the gravest external danger that ever threatened it. Was it likely, the common man wondered, that he could now turn himself in a moment from the triumphant victor into a patient radical reformer of the social and economic life of the nation? Was it not wiser to leave this to the milder talents of a modest politician, who from his manhood up had devoted himself to the rights and well-being of the underprivileged classes, the leader, moreover, of a party pledged unequivocally to social reform?

It may be, in fact, that no elections are won by the exercise of personality, by the magnetism of a particular man, though they can perhaps be lost by a lack of it. In most of the elections in my life-time the divisions between the main parties have been fairly clear-cut. They were crystal clear in 1910 when Asquith and Balfour, coat-tails flying, were racing each other up those ladders of electoral results; much less clear in 1964 when the Tory Party seemed to choose a leader as like in many respects to the leader of the Socialists as they could get, and the deep and crucial issue of the day—entry into the European Economic Community—cut right across party lines and was never put to the electorate at all. But in 1910 the Liberal measures of taxation and national insurance, blocked by the unbridled powers of the House of Lords, and Home Rule for Ireland, were political issues so profoundly felt that they separated friends and divided families. Nor could anybody confuse the voice, the appearance and the manner of Asquith with those of Balfour—the grave and measured tones, the classic style, the calm Olympian self-confidence of the one, and the indifferent charm and languid detachment of the other. Asquith, in peace-time at any rate, had an unrivalled grasp of the political issues of his day; he was the unquestioned leader of his highly talented Cabinet—perhaps the strongest ever—and the weight of his eloquence dominated the House of Commons. It was a travesty to depict him as the shuffling indecisive man and to pin upon him out of context the dilatory label of 'wait and see'—more unfair even than the damaging cliché, 'You've never had it so good' dragged from its place, deprived of its sequel and hung like an albatross around Harold Macmillan's neck. Balfour no doubt was more effective than he allowed people to imagine and in the midst of his airy philosophising he must have had a realistic and decisive touch. But he invited anecdotes by his vague, abstracted, unambitious temperament. On a Foreign Office memorandum, presenting two alternative courses for his decision, he is reported to have written, 'yes'. Late in life he is alleged to have begun some public speech with flippant disdain, 'When I was Prime Minister or something of that sort . . .' But it cannot be true that he once enquired 'What is the Balfour Declaration and why is it so named?'

These two men, Asquith and Balfour, were the protagonists when I was a boy and naturally I can know nothing about them at first hand. I am not sure that I ever saw Balfour and certainly I never heard him speak. Of Asquith I had an early glimpse. Some time in the first half of 1914, I took my place as usual in the choir of Canterbury Cathedral at Saturday Evensong. I was a probationer scholar at the King's School, aged about 12, and one of the checks to what might, most improbably, have been incipient intellectual pride was the obligation to attend this Saturday service in the middle of a precious half-holiday and to kneel unsupported by desk or rail under the baleful eye of old Dean Wace. It was a dutiful observance and no more; and little is remembered now of these penitentiary Saturdays except the disturbance caused on this particular day by the late entry into the high stalls in front of me of the Prime Minister himself, accompanied by one of his private secretaries and by a woman who to my young eyes seemed smart and beautiful beyond the common. I later learnt that she was Mrs Winston Churchill. This was an exciting intrusion into our regular and regimented lives, my first glimpse of a prominent national figure then at the zenith of his powers, before the alarming complexities of total war demanded from him qualities of leadership which he did not possess and before the horror of the war shattered his nervous powers by the death in action of his brilliant eldest son. Asquith was to remain for me something of a hero. In the long contest with Lloyd George I gave him my young and inexperienced sympathy. I thought of him, as I toiled through the orthodox labours of a classical education, as the eloquent mouthpiece of liberal ideas and my speeches at the Radley College Debating Society were decorated with phrases plucked from a publication of the time, *The Pocket Asquith*. When I was at Merton he was living at Sutton Courtenay and was an occasional visitor to the College; and it seemed to me and to many of my friends a shabby piece of political jobbery when he was denied the Chancellorship of the University. But he was a politician and like all politicians was ambitious for power and not over-scrupulous about the methods he employed to obtain it and to keep it. He believed, in the professional style of all his breed, that he was better equipped to exercise that power for the public good than anybody else; and that is the spur and the motive which move most men to enter this violently competitive world. How few succeed and how few are remembered!

Most men of my age would find it difficult to name more than one or two of the members of Asquith's Cabinet in 1914 and the truth is that with very few exceptions it is only the Prime Ministers who outlast their lifetime. Lloyd George was a member of that famous group, but he displaced his own chief and brought us to victory in 1918. Winston Churchill, it may surprise younger men to know, was also a member of that very liberal Liberal Administration but his fame rests upon more splendid and more heroic achievements. For the rest who but the political historian remembers, and who cares? Yet over a spread of more than fifty years a great many men of all ages and all types, advancing with courageous excitement in a much-nursed constituency to the top of the poll, have entered the House of Commons and taken the oath with the valiant intention of righting social injustices and leading their country to heights of progress and glory never before attained. But the hero of the hustings finds soon enough that he must cool his heels on the back benches for many years to come. Yet still he looks for power to carry out his grand designs. There is no sense of power where he sits. At last some exalted Minister, listening by chance and not design to one of his carefully devised speeches or finding him to be a convivial member of his club, casts a favourable glance upon him and invites him to be his Parliamentary Private Secretary. Now at last he has his foot on the ladder, but in a few months the top rungs of the ladder are far out of sight again and, as he carries question and answer, suggestion and counter-suggestion from the Minister on the front bench to the permanent civil servants in the official box at the back of the House, he wonders more than ever where the source of power is, certainly not in him, the humble transmitter of ministerial anxiety and confident official response.

He is a junior Minister now, a step nearer the realisa-tion of his ambition, a Parliamentary Under-Secretary, the deputy, the alter ego, as he hopes, of a Cabinet Minister. The bright prospect is soon obscured by the heavy clouds of depart-mental procedures. He is comparatively young and inexperienced, he must be tutored and protected by the wise old civil servants who do not come and go and never make mistakes. They are courteous to him, they cherish him but there are some things he must not know and cannot handle. These are for the Minister alone, Cabinet secrets outside his ken, beyond his grasp. Meanwhile it is his task to wind up for the Government on the second reading of the Bill for the control of the discharge into rivers of effluent from industrial concerns and to make a speech at the week-end on behalf of the Minister at the annual reunion of warehousemen at Llandudno. Is power then a mirage, can he never lay hands upon it?

At last he is a Minister. Faithful devotion to the Party, industrious attention to the details of some particular subject or group of subjects, the surrender of strongly-held private opinions in deference to the official view, and some sensitive attentions to the personal whims and wishes of his leader have brought him in the fulness of time to a seat in the Cabinet, surely the true centre of power. A Minister has power, it is certain, but power of a particular yet restricted kind. In his own Department he is lord and master, his slightest wish noted and acted upon without delay. The Minister does not like to see bicycles left in the hall, his tea must be weak, he must not be disturbed between 5 p.m. and 6 p.m. except by the Prime Minister himself, the windows must be left open when he is out of the room, minutes submitted to him must be presented in a certain way and so on. All this is quite right and proper. He has a burden to carry and should not be worried by small irritations. His private secretaries will soon grow used to his foibles and will gain some satisfaction from the exercise of their puny authority in seeing that they are respected. He has real power too. Now at last he is the Head of a Department, the problems of which he has for many patient years studied with assiduous care. He has plenty of ideas about new policies, he would like to see a new approach and other methods tried. He is eager to begin and his first weeks of power are spent in deep discussion with the Permanent Secretary of the Department, that wise old civil servant, and his chief assistants. It is perhaps a little damping and a little mortifying to the Minister to find that all his new ideas seem to have been tested and examined years before and in most cases found to be impracticable for this reason or for that. Obstacles and objections confront and hamper his enthusiasm at every turn. But still, he takes heart from the conviction that he has the country's mandate for his opinions and that though civil servants have a duty to point out the difficulties, they must in the end be overruled and ordered to conform to the sovereign will of the people. But the weight of Civil Service opinion—'heavy as frost and deep almost as life'—is not the only curb upon his initiative. He is, of course, responsible to Parliament for all the acts of his Department. He must at all times be ready to defend them against the hostilities and suspicions of back-bench members and patiently to answer Parliamentary Questions cunningly devised to embarrass and confuse him. Too much of his time and the time of his officials is spent in this unproductive combat and too little on the preparation of those reforming policies so dear to his heart. Then again he is a member of the Cabinet and shares with other Cabinet Ministers collective responsibility for the policies of the Government as a whole. He must make sure at all stages of the formulation of his particular policy that the Prime Minister feels that there is no conflict here with other departmental policies and that it can be comprehended within the Government's legislative programme. This is no easy task. Other Ministers have their ewe lambs too, and they are all busy whispering allurements in the Prime Minister's ear, and of course if expenditure of public money is involved the Chancellor of the Exchequer must be brought at least to agree in principle, before the proposals are put to the Cabinet at all. It is a long, laborious way, full of twists and turns and set-backs. The fact is that the press of immediate events, a war in the Middle East, a seamen's strike, a dangerous menace to the pound sterling, the hi-jacking of an aeroplane, together with the tortuous and time-consuming procedures of Parliament, make it very difficult for any Government, whatever its majority, to put through more than a half-dozen major pieces of legislation within its statutory span of life.

Is he satisfied, then, with his situation as a Minister? Is this power enough for him, this little peck of power, clipped, truncated and confined? There is only one step more. If he is not satisfied yet, he must jostle and fight until he has achieved the dominating position of Leader and Prime Minister. It *is* a dominating position. There is no doubt about the supremacy of the Prime Minister in the British political scene. There may be no constitutional justification for this, but it is an undeniable fact; and that perhaps is why it is Prime Ministers alone who are remembered. The individual Cabinet Minister who goes no higher makes little enough impact and will be forgotten unless perhaps he has been the centre of some public scandal

—some Crichel Down, some Christine Keeler. Exceptions of course there are and more particularly in the realm of foreign affairs—Edward Grey, the lean aristocrat who spoke for Britain in 1914, even Curzon, the last of the insufferables, and certainly Ernie Bevin, the large-hearted, heavy-handed West Countryman who presented a much truer and profounder picture of England to the world of 1945 and dominated with unlettered wisdom and rough spontaneous humour the first efforts for the reconstruction of Western Europe.

John Simon held almost every important office, except that of Prime Minister, in an extended political career. He was never a popular figure and was the victim of one of Lloyd George's sharpest comments, 'John Simon has sat so long upon the fence that the iron has entered into his soul.' Aneurin Bevan had a flair, a touch of genius and a spell-binding eloquence, equalled only by his fellow-countryman Lloyd George, but he will be remembered for his personal gifts, his tempestuous and rebellious nature, rather than for his pioneering of the National Health Service. It was Winston Churchill's opinion that he would in the end achieve the leadership of the Socialist Party. Death ruled otherwise and removed with undiscriminating blow both leader and strongest rival, opening an easy and unexpected path for the restless ambition of another. Perhaps Lord Butler will be remembered, the professional runner-up, the assiduous stand-in, the best Prime Minister we never had.

Prime Ministers are remembered because of their unquestioned supremacy over their colleagues and because all the acts and events of their Premiership are conveniently classified under their names. Asquith emasculated the House of Lords and introduced Home Rule for Ireland. Lloyd George won the war. The contributions of other Ministers towards winning that war are largely forgotten. Lloyd George was the leader; he won it, and certainly we never looked like winning it before he ousted Asquith from the premier place. He gave a fresh impulse to the whole thing, he put his finger into everybody's pie, he let no one go to sleep on his job. He was lucky, doubly lucky, that the chance catastrophes of war had put an end to the immovable obstinacy and secretiveness of Lord Kitchener and that he himself—contrary to what was originally intended

—had not accompanied him in that ill-fated ship. He was the first Prime Minister in recent times to feel that it was his duty to interfere with the generals and admirals and to question the wisdom of their strategy, a subject which professional military men were determined to regard as beyond the wit and understanding of the lay mind. Asquith had never really felt that his responsibility extended so far, but Churchill, who shared and applauded these bold incursions, was to establish a far greater extension of these particular frontiers of a Prime Minister's responsibility in the Second World War. There is a good precedent for this after all; Chatham, I believe, wrote with his own hand the directive to Wolfe for the capture of Quebec. No historian will attempt to deprive Lloyd George of the major praise for our victory in 1918; and not even his own sorry performance thereafter can obliterate from the hearts of those who lived through those days the feelings of pride and gratitude for the courageous resilience and spell-binding eloquence of the little long-haired Welsh Wizard. Perhaps he had enjoyed too much power in those war years when curbs and checks on power are somewhat relaxed and the nation is united by a single aim. An overweening self-confidence and a certain laxity in his private life seemed gradually to rob him of his political sense and to undermine his popular support. The eloquence remained. I heard him once, in the Town Hall at Oxford some time in the twenties. I was an Asquithian Liberal and hostile to the very name of Lloyd George. I went to jeer and despise but the wit and charm of his eloquence bound me in a spell—until I got home and realised how little he had said of any consequence at all. The decline of Lloyd George was almost pitiable. From the General Election of 1922 until his death in 1945 it had always seemed, especially in the dreadful decade of the thirties, that he might somehow make a comeback and galvanise us once more, but the spirit was lacking and often his opinions were ill-founded, wrong-headed, even pusillanimous. Lloyd George certainly loved power, more perhaps than most politicians. From 1916 to 1918 he experienced as full a flavour of it as can ever have been the lot of an Englishman. In peace-time the flavour was by comparison insipid and his glittering career drifted away in disappointment. Once the most brilliant opportunist in our political history, his sense of timing now deserted him. He followed up his castigation of Chamberlain's handling of Mussolini with extravagant praise of Hitler and a hopelessly wrong estimate of his ambitions. When at long last Chamberlain had set his powers to waging the war, Lloyd George was in favour of temporising and parley.

'Tranquillity' was the strange watch-word of his successor as Prime Minister in 1922. At that time Lloyd George scoffed at this faint-hearted appeal to the electorate, but it had its attraction for war-weary disillusioned men and Bonar Law, with no gifts of leadership at all, reigned briefly in No. 10. The complex moves and counter-moves, the modest disclaimers and confident advances, the conversations in this private house and that London club, the confused pattern of intrigue, which finally brought this humdrum, humourless, pessimistic Scot to break the Coalition at a famous meeting in the Carlton Club make up a far more fantastic political melodrama than the comings and goings, the visitings, the despatch of messages and the telephone calls which disturbed the sick bed of Harold Macmillan in Sister Agnes' Nursing Home in 1963 and yet gave him a sense of power retained even as power left him. This mysterious caballing and conspiring seems to be one of the attractions of politics, and for all the democratic processes by which both major political parties now elect their leader the corridor-whispering and backstairs impulses will be no whit diminished. The dark curtain which seeks to hide the stealthy thrusts of jealous and ambitious men exists no doubt in other walks of life and in the university world has been torn aside by the imaginative hand of C. P. Snow. But as politics is the pursuit of power over a whole nation, the competition is wider and the rivalry more intense. It is doubtful, however, if poor Bonar Law felt any sense of triumph or power as a result of that famous meeting in the Carlton Club which finally sent him to sit isolated, indeterminate and ill for a few unhappy months in Downing Street. A fatal and suffocating illness forced his urgent resignation and deprived the King of his Prime Minister's advice on the question of a successor. King George V, acting as usual with strict attention to constitutional propriety and with a pretty shrewd idea of popular opinion, sent for Stanley Baldwin, then Chancellor of the Exchequer.

Lord Curzon, who had been waiting with arrogant assumption and absolute confidence for the royal summons, hid his mortification behind a display of contempt for the King's ineptitude. This was a real blow for Curzon, who above all politicians of his time, loved power with a passionate devotion, loved it for its own sake and for all its gorgeous trappings and took inhuman delight in the obsequious attentions which it can command.

When I was in my twenties, an impoverished schoolmaster, still unsure of my vocation and unjustifiably confident of untested powers, I fancied myself as a politician and sought about, not very hopefully, for some method of standing for Parliament. It was really a lost cause before I began, because the nursing of constituencies and the fighting of elections take up professional time and no man could combine this skirmishing on the outskirts of a political life with a proper attention to professional duty. In consequence I made but a brief foray, spending some part of my holidays in helping the Liberal candidate in a pre-election campaign in the Vale of Evesham. I toured around making tedious and thoughtful speeches to gatherings of middle-aged women and a few superannuated men in village halls, my youthful confidence and enthusiasm ebbing away as I felt the dull and uncomprehending stare of my exiguous audience exercising a blight upon me. I attended local Liberal socials and dances, which in fact had no real connection with any form of politics at all, interrupting the gay proceedings with an unwelcome political speech carefully timed to end with a glowing encomium of the candidate, who, thus heralded, appeared at my side accompanied by a chorus of a dozen pretty girls, picked from the locality for their natural ability to attract all masculine eyes to the stage on which the candidate now smilingly occupied the central place. I began to wonder uncertainly whether this sort of thing was any more to my taste than hammering Latin grammar into dunderheads, but on the candidate's advice I went with his introduction to the Liberal Party Headquarters in Abingdon Street, where I had a brief interview with Herbert Samuel. What I lacked was experience, he told me with obvious truth, and there could of course be no safe, or indeed marginal, seat for a novice with no money. The thing to do was to fight a hopeless seat against some Tory giant and if I succeeded in reducing his majority by even a thousand or two, I should have come through a testing time and begun to make a name for myself. This seemed to me very sound practical advice and, when he went on to say that, if I were game, he might be able to get me adopted as the Liberal candidate in the Bewdley constituency, I began to fancy myself as a young and shining David nimbly assaulting the ponderous complacency of Goliath Baldwin. But it was not to be. There was no possible way for me to combine politics with the earning of a living. I went back to my gown and my blackboard, fell in love with the schoolmaster's art, and had no more parliamentary longings in me.

Nevertheless I still cherish some regrets about my retreat from this unequal contest. I should have had no chance, of course, no chance at all, but I might have learned something of the inner workings of this strange individual and of the motive force which kept him in or very near the highest seats of power for about a dozen years. Did he share with other politicians the love of power and the belief in his own paramount ability to exercise it, or was he in fact the plain pipe-smoking Englishman called from his family industry, his patrimony and his friends to a service which he did not seek but which his sense of duty could not refuse? To doubt the sincerity of the man is not possible. Only once, I think, did I hear him speak and that was at the Canning Club in Oxford. I thought him dull and heavy, but reading again, as I have recently, his collected speeches, *On England*, I was struck— as most of us were at the time—by the deep love he felt for the fields, the hills, the houses, the men and women of this island, their customs and traditions and the ancient disciplines of education. He wanted to realise an England at peace with itself, contented, industrious and prosperous, submitting with confidence and affection to a paternal government exercised with clemency and compassion by men of broad education and sensitive hearts. He thought he was well qualified to lead a Government of this kind and he was probably right. Men trusted him even when his methods failed; or perhaps it was that he had no methods. He hoped that by his humane precept and example masters and men would love each other and bring the country to unknown heights of industrial progress and strength. Yet for all his pleas, keenly felt and warmly applauded by all classes of society, the country suffered in his time the paralysis of the general strike and the dead hand of widespread unemployment. For foreign affairs and defence he had less feeling, perhaps, than any other Prime Minister of this century. It was a very fine thing, he said, to have pacts of friendship and alliance with other nations and it was right to seek international peace and ensue it. He wished successive Foreign Secretaries good luck in their pursuit. His priority, he made clear, was peace at home, peace in industry, peace and friendship between all classes of society. His detachment from external problems seemed to increase with time and led him to a dangerous indifference to foreign threats and a seeming neglect of essential self-defence. He sought escape from blame with another of those fatal phrases which fall from the politician's unwary tongue and 'old sealed lips', he became the Prime Minister who dared not tell the truth about the national defences and ask for a mandate to put them right, because, if he had done so, he would have lost the Election. His great negative success was his handling of the abdication of Edward VIII and it is certain that, if there had to be an abdication, no other politician of the time could have handled it with the same sensitive tact or in a more tranquillising bedside manner. There was no upsurge of feeling, no riot, no serious faction of King's friends, hardly a ripple of disturbance in the ordered life of Baldwin's England. For all the tranquillising effects of his influence and his personality he remains a controversial figure and still stands at the bar of history. Was he negligent to the point of culpability in respect of our foreign and defence policy, or was he, as his latest defenders assert, so long-sighted as to see that, whatever the state of our defences might be, the only thing that would count in the inevitable war just around the corner was the morale and the unity of our people? If he really thought so far ahead he was right and it is beyond question that if we had been a seriously divided nation we should have been annihilated by the disaster of Dunkirk. For myself I doubt if any man could have enjoyed such a cunning and calculated prescience, but it can of course be said without fear of contradiction that what Baldwin cared for most was the unity of England. I doubt very much if he thought of this unity in terms of a united front of courage and endurance against a foreign aggressor. The ideal he cherished was a unity of sympathy and friendship between all classes in our own island —the artisans, the professionals and the capitalists working together in active harmony for the economic success and the social happiness of our own country. He looked no further than that. The indivisible front of boldness and tenacity which we presented to the world in 1940 was the result of many historical and contemporary factors. If Baldwin's political achievement was one of these, so also was the obstinate failure of Neville Chamberlain whose misconceived foreign policy in peace and inept conduct of the war united Englishmen in exasperated impatience and a determination that he should make way for someone who really knew how to speak and act for England.

The performance of politicians in the dreadful decade of the thirties was a very uninspiring one. Those who fought their way into the seats of power made very ineffective use of the power they had achieved and those who opposed them were disparate and disunited. If Churchill's voice was a constant scourge to the blind and complacent foreign policy of Neville Chamberlain, he failed to rally the full support of those who thought like him on this question because they were alienated by what seemed to them the wrong-headed prejudice of his opinions on India. Anthony Eden, having at long last extricated himself from his wholly false position as Chamberlain's Foreign Secretary, was flat and ineffective in opposition. Throughout the decade three men shared the supreme power—Ramsay Macdonald, Stanley Baldwin and Neville Chamberlain. Ramsay Macdonald, once thought by some to be a dynamic fire-eating revolutionary, the terror of the Establishment, was burnt out and seemed to have sold himself to the aristocracy and to be lost in vague and meaningless generalities. When Leader of the Socialist Government of 1929 he had failed to deal with the mounting problem of unemployment and he did no better when he found himself in 1931 at the head of a so-called National Government with a majority so fat that it was unable to act incisively in any direction. Unemployment increased daily and reached desperate proportions in certain areas of the country; at one time, for example, thirty-five per cent of the insured population of West Cumberland was out of work. It is true the Government passed the Special Areas Act which gave them some rather inadequate powers to deal with this cancer but even these they did not fully use. The Prime Minister went about the country, handsome, dignified and earnest, but his magnetism had gone. The working man turned away and the majority party in the House of Commons had hardly stopped acclaiming the patriotism and nobility of this leonine figure before it began to scoff and deride. It was not surprising that a Prime Minister who habitually took refuge in meaningless jumbles of words, whose only aim was to convey a vague and foolish optimism about subjects which the Government seemed powerless to handle, should have been contemptuously styled by Churchill 'the boneless wonder on the Treasury bench'. What could be thought of a national leader who thus expressed himself on the bitter subject of unemployment:— 'As to the treatment of the unemployed . . . the issue lies between those who are working at the problem in detail and those who are not working at it at all but speaking about it and throwing sniffs of red herrings, like the abolition of any form of means test, under the noses of hard-stricken people . . .' or who rallied the Geneva Conference on Disarmament in 1933 with this inspiring message:—". . . Great words and great phrases like justice and so on very often mean nothing and have serpents concealed in their folds . . .'

Since the publication of Lord Moran's book on Churchill there has been a good deal of discussion about the health of Prime Ministers and the need to ensure, in the public interest, that they are physically capable of carrying the enormous burden laid upon them. No sensible or trustworthy procedure has so far been suggested for bringing this about. It would be strange indeed if a panel of doctors should be entrusted with the task of deciding whether the man selected by the Sovereign and the people to lead the country was, or was not, capable of fulfilling his task. This would be an exercise of power never contemplated by Aristotle and not so far claimed by the British Medical Association. Yet it is, I think, quite certain that the nervous and physical energy of Ramsay Macdonald in 1931 was inadequate for the task he took on. Asquith, as I have pointed out, was physically and nervously incapable of carrying the additional burdens, both public and private, which the war laid upon him. Bonar Law was a dying man when he took office and Neville Chamberlain's power of making confident judgments and pushing them through against weighty advice had by 1939 been much diminished by the inroads of the disease which killed him in November, 1940. There are many who think Churchill's last Premiership is better forgotten— the uncertain fumbling of an old man striving against senility —and the extinguishing in the tragic smoke of Suez of Eden's once-glittering star is a tragedy of decay, physical and temperamental.

It ought to be safe enough to leave it to the politician. If he does not feel capable of doing the job then surely he will decline the Sovereign's request to form a Government? But he never does; and once upon a time the Cabinet waited and waited through long and tedious sessions of frustrated expectation before its senior member was at last able to take from his pocket a manuscript, yellowed with age and much dog-eared, and read out in the Cabinet Room a tribute, composed long before, to the erstwhile powers of Gladstone, now positively making his last appearance. Men who love power are most reluctant to surrender it and continue to think that they can exercise it better than anyone else; in the forefront of this group stands the politician.

Ramsay Macdonald, at least, voluntarily withdrew from the leadership he had long since ceased to exercise before death overtook him, and retired into private life, hated by his former colleagues who were convinced that he had betrayed his principles and his past and derided by his new supporters who now viewed him with a half-amused and half-affectionate contempt. I remember well that when I reported his sudden death during a trans-Atlantic crossing to my mother she exhibited her habitual distrustful contempt for politicians by replying 'I wish it had been Lloyd George; at least poor old Ramsay was doing no harm.' That was a somewhat poignant epitaph for a politician whose love of power and personal vanity had brought him from the dangerous and precipitous heights of revolutionary fervour to an incoherent confusion of mind and a relaxed surrender to the social embraces of the upper classes. But then my mother, I think, would have subscribed to the opinion of a learned foreign observer on the pathology of party government : 'To the low types which the human race has produced from Cain down to Tartuffe, the age of democracy has added a new one—the politician.'

For myself the hero-worship of my early years—the admiration for Asquith, the deification of Woodrow Wilson—gave place by degrees to a maturer judgment, which no longer expected perfection in men, and finally to a deep respect for the confident demeanour of the politician, his astonishing resilience, his unflinching endurance of fatigue, his armour against misrepresentation and personal abuse. From time to time, of course, I felt affection also, but mostly I think for those who had given up the pursuit of power and looked on with a relaxed wisdom at the feverish goings-on of the occupants of the front bench. 'It is all very well,' one of my close friends once said to me, 'if you like the silly pomp and ceremony, the ringing tones of the toastmaster—"Pray silence for the Right Honourable - - -, a Knight Commander of the most Excellent Order, etc. etc."—but if you don't want these antiquated absurdities, you must satisfy yourself either by achieving the premier place, or, if you can't do that, by retiring to a position of amused detachment.' That was an engaging comment, but there are, of course, politicians who cannot be put into any of those three classes—the Prime Minister class, the pomposity class or the detached observer. There was, for example, Ernest Bevin. It was only the war which brought him into politics at all. Until then he had been a great trade union leader whose power, based on the votes of his members, extended beyond the satisfaction of their particular needs and desires into the wider world of industrial relations and the national responsibilities of organised labour. He became an indispensable member of the war-time Coalition as Minister of Labour and of Attlee's post-war Government as Foreign Secretary, but he was never a politician in the ordinary sense of the word. He could intrigue and manœuvre in his own trade union world, but the intrigues and manœuvres of politicians attracted only his disdain and his anger. He was not ambitious to be the leader and he treated with crushing contempt those who tried to involve him. He enjoyed, I have no doubt, the real power which office gave him but he exercised it with his eyes fixed exclusively upon the national interest as seen from that office. He was not looking for a chance to reach the summit himself. He was concerned only with the proper organization of manpower in war and the most effective foreign policy for this country in peace. It would be harsh and unjust to suggest that most politicians are not thinking of the national interest. They certainly are, but they are thinking also, as Bevin never had occasion to do, of their careers. They entered politics in order to get to the top, and that after all is the objective of most men in all careers. They want the top position because they believe that in that position they can exercise the most powerful influence for the country's good. Uncle Ernie did not think like this, because he was not a political careerist and was entirely satisfied with the exercise of the particular authority which had been allotted to him. He was, however, ruthlessly determined to defend the seats of power, which he and his friends occupied, against the incursions of politicians for whom he had a personal distrust or dislike. 'You should be more considerate,' one of his friends once urged, 'after all Nye Bevan is his own worst enemy.' 'No, he bloody well isn't,' Uncle Ernie retorted, 'not as long as I'm alive.' That is severe and probably misguided—much more so than his often expressed determination that Herbert Morrison should become Foreign Secretary only over his dead body. In this opinion he was right and proved right by Morrison's lamentable performance in that role. It was also a sadly prophetic dictum. Ernie Bevin persevered in this exacting office long after his health had failed, because he was inwardly convinced that Britain would suffer less from his increasingly nerveless touch than from Morrison's cockney self-confidence. I saw him often in the throes of this last struggle, distressingly overweight and short of breath, carrying his great body with halting difficulty about his daily tasks, nursing his old head until he could wheeze out his still decisive opinions.

In a different category again, and in a different age, was F. E. Smith, later Earl of Birkenhead. He was perhaps the most talented man of his time, at Oxford finely distinguished in the Schools and in the athletic world, good-looking, gay and attractively lawless, at the Bar a brilliant advocate and in politics the bright young hope of the Tory Party. His career brought him to the Lord Chancellorship but the mischances

33

of political life prevented him from ever attaining the leadership of his party. In the break-up of the Coalition in 1922 he had thrown in his lot with Lloyd George and after the substantial victory of the Conservative Party at the General Election he must have viewed his political future with grave misgiving.

In his early years he had been a Prize Fellow of Merton and he had always retained a keen interest in the College. In the summer of 1923 it was generally believed among the undergraduates at Merton, that, having reached a political impasse, he would not disdain an invitation to become Warden. How much truth there was in this belief I have no idea and in any case there were two major obstacles to be surmounted. A number of the Fellows had no great love for him, and the reigning Warden, Thomas Bowman, showed no inclination whatever to remove his gloomy presence from his gloomy house and to lift from the College the dark shadow of his disagreeable and parsimonious personality. In fact he did not retire for another ten or fifteen years. All the same we held to our belief and it seemed to us to be somewhat confirmed when the great man let it be known that he would welcome an invitation to dine with our undergraduate dining club, the Myrmidon Club. Lord Birkenhead was, at first, a little stiff and we, for all our adolescent arrogance, were somewhat in awe of him. With plentiful brandy and good cigars he grew more mellow and we grew less timid and self-conscious. I felt, as we all did, the varied strength of his personality, but the most lasting impression made on my young feelings was of his unbounded egoism and conceit.

These are not necessarily the attributes of successful politicians, although the fierce competition in which they spend their lives, the effusive adulation with which their supporters enclose them, and the uplifted sense of public duty which, I suppose, encourages them, must put in their daily path temptations to a self-confident vanity. Temptations of this kind occur in many other walks of life—the professional cricketer or footballer, playing his game for the delight, as he is constantly told, of the vast British public, admired, embraced and made to feel that his mere signature will console large sections of the adolescent population; the actor, as I have said, preening himself upon his fan mail, in constant expectation that he will catch the attentive eye of the theatre-goer; the schoolmaster and university don; the clergyman even, pleased with his pulpit and the admiration of his captive flock. All these are just as vain as most politicians. Indeed I am not sure that personal vanity is a very common characteristic of the latter. Ramsay Macdonald certainly had it and it was, I fancy, the besetting weakness of Anthony Eden. For all his charm and his good looks he was not immediately attractive to talk to. In company, such attention as he gave you was wandering and uncertain, his eye constantly alert to light upon someone more important or more adulatory than yourself. His appearance, which could safely have been left to its naturally handsome devices, occupied too much of his anxiety. What sort of a figure was he cutting? What were people thinking about him? Were they subject to his charm? Attlee cared for none of these things, had no vanity at all and, partly in consequence perhaps, no personal charm. I never thought that Churchill suffered from this form of vanity. He was not much interested in appearances, but he was without question a selfish actor who wanted the centre of the stage. It is now well known that conversation often took the form of a monologue and attempts to interject were roughly brushed aside. It was very rash indeed to volunteer a story in his presence. Its flow was interrupted by bored interrogations —'Well?' 'What is the point of that?' and so on—and its end marked by contemptuous silence. I only once had a private meal with Churchill and that was in his state-room in the *Queen Mary* on our way home from America in January, 1952. He was genial and expansive and the drift of the conversation encouraged me to tell him a little story about Dick Stokes who had been Minister of Works in Attlee's Government. A cormorant had taken up an unusual and unexpected domicile in St James's Park and was consorting with the three pelicans; this unusual cohabitation did not last long because the Minister of Works got up one morning in a proprietary mood and shot the cormorant. The direct reaction to this piece of information was negative, neither amused nor hostile, but it prompted the recitation of quite a long poem about St James's Park which he had read in *Punch* years before and remembered without difficulty. I suppose Harold Macmillan

35

had his share of vanity but it was never obtrusive and if he liked you he set up no barriers at all.

These are the four Prime Ministers—Churchill, Attlee, Eden and Macmillan—of whom I know something at first hand, but not very much of Eden. I have written about them elsewhere. In the context of this book I look at them again to see how far they exemplify the theory that men are led into a political career by an invincible desire for power, power over the lives of others, power over the destinies of nations. If, in fact, they share this attribute it is not altogether to their discredit. They want power but they want it for a creditable reason. They want it because they feel they can use it to better purpose than anybody else. This is the justification for what sometimes seems the squalid intrigue of party politics, the cunning, even deceitful, manœuvres, the scoring of points at random, with no holds barred. The end justifies the means if the end is office and the assumption of power. This is the theme of *The Endless Adventure* by F. S. Oliver, that penetrating and graphic history of politics in the eighteenth century, the everlasting comings and goings, the bribes and the corruption— all excused by this conviction that power is far better in my hands than in yours. It was the underlying reason for Disraeli's Reform Bill of 1867. He was not greatly concerned about the contents of the Bill itself but, in Robert Blake's words, 'wanted to pass a Bill, do down Gladstone and Russell, and stay in power'. And his Tory supporters, who in their hearts feared and hated reform, were so elated by the victory over Gladstone, that they drank a toast 'to the man who rode the race, who took the time, who kept the time, and who did the trick'. It is very hard, sometimes, in contemplating the moves and counter-moves of party political life to avoid the suspicion that in the inexorable and unprincipled pursuit of power the national good is occasionally overlooked.

There can be no doubt at all that Churchill loved power and his detractors would say that he turned his coat in order to regain it. The young and brilliant Liberal hope, probably the natural successor to Asquith and Lloyd George if the Liberal Party had remained a powerful unity, picked his way over their wrangling postures through a flimsy staging post of so-called Constitutionalism into the Tory fastness as Baldwin's

Chancellor of the Exchequer in 1925. But this indictment cannot be sustained because he was out of office from 1929 to 1939, belabouring the Government for its Indian policy and castigating it for its neglect of defence and its appeasement of dictators. Only the war brought him back into office, too late now to make preparations against it but not too late to save his country from destruction and to guide it to final victory. For him this was the full measure of power, the power to direct a united nation with a single aim, a power much vaster than the power of a peace-time Prime Minister with a majority in the House of Commons, a power carrying with it the awesome responsibility for the lives and deaths of countless men and women and for the dissolution or survival of nations and empires. It had no terrors for Churchill who wrote with convincing candour:

'. . . as I went to bed at about 3 a.m. [11 May, 1940] I was conscious of a profound sense of relief. At last I had the authority to give directions over the whole scene. I felt as if I were walking with destiny, and that all my past life had been but a preparation for this hour and for this trial.'

The power was now his and he exercised it relentlessly and tirelessly for five years. Not for one moment of health, or even half-health, did he spare himself, and if he was conscious of the lordly power now in his grasp, he was even more conscious of the responsibilities which beset him, lay in bed with him, walked or sat beside him every fleeting leisure hour, and stood a watchful and exacting sentinel behind his chair of state. It was this combination in him—the pervasive sense of responsibility and the absolute confidence in his own powers—which made him interfering, obtrusive, remorseless, inconsiderate, which impelled him to follow up every enterprise, every project, every plan, every enquiry in the smallest detail, demanding immediate answers to impossible questions. He was ultimately responsible; if the thing went wrong, it was his fault. He could not just give an order and leave it alone; if the order was inefficiently carried out, the failure was his. Besides, he knew better than anyone else how to do it; he was 'walking with destiny', and destiny knew more than Cabinet Ministers and Chiefs of Staff. To convince him that he might be mistaken needed much expenditure of midnight oil, long and fevered hours of disputation, frayed tempers and hurt feelings, and, if he finally gave way, it was without any admission of defeat, let alone apology, just a grumpy acquiescence and a swift recourse, not retreat, to the next battlefield. He was responsible and he had the power; and so, in the context of an all-out war, he could not behave otherwise. No other English politician alive or dead would have seen his duty in this comprehensive all-absorbing way—not even Lloyd George, I think, and certainly not Asquith, who was content to let his colleagues and his Service chiefs get on with their jobs. They were grateful for that, but it was a mistake. If the Chiefs of Staff and Commanders-in-Chief might have been grateful for rather fewer of Churchill's nagging and sometimes irrelevant admonishments, they would have been the first to admit that these immediate and searching inquisitions not only kept them on their toes but gave special impetus and urgency to the mighty machines over which they presided. In the whole history of England I doubt if any other single individual ever exercised such direct and incessant control over the nation's affairs—except, perhaps, Oliver Cromwell, who in devotion to the cause and utter absorption was the equal of Churchill. But Oliver played out his tragic part upon a much smaller stage, and in the enjoyment of power was tortured and reluctant, while Churchill woke every morning with renewed feelings of excitement and delight. The garish dressing-gowns, the fancy slippers, the grotesque head-gear, the topsy-turvy way of life, the afternoon sleep and waking midnight hours, the rudeness, the exactions, the pouting sulks and sentimental tears, the imperial attitude, the terse injunctions to the bedside courtiers, the bulldog snarl at unfriendly foreigners or inefficient public servants, the endless monologues over interminable dinners, the occasional relaxation, a battle at bezique or a very late-night film—these were the fruits of power, the oddly assorted rewards for the selfless expenditure of all his nervous energy and matchless experience and ability in the service of his country.

Attlee could never have been a great war-time Prime Minister and had he been called upon would not have enjoyed it. It would have been a colourless and unimaginative performance of duty, without drive and without gusto. I suppose that Churchill and Attlee were about the same height, but whereas it seems quite appropriate to attribute to Churchill 'the imperial stature, the colossal stride' and to tremble at 'the keen threatenings of that fulgent eye,' such descriptions of Attlee would seem far-fetched to the point of absurdity. The motives of the two men, also, must have been totally different —Churchill born into the traditional ranks of power, the descendant of one of the truly great figures in English history, by birth and background naturally disposed towards a political career, Attlee coming from a good professional family with high standards of conduct, not connected in any way with the ruling families which dominated political life in the nineteenth and early twentieth centuries, liberally educated as men of that class were, unpretentious, unambitious. Attlee's motive in entering politics was an acute consciousness of social injustice and inequality. It was in Parliament, he thought, that he might find opportunities to put this right, at least to ameliorate the squalid lot of the East-Enders, whom in his early manhood he had tried to serve. He never fancied himself as a war-time leader and I doubt if he even supposed for a moment that he would ever lead his party, let alone become Prime Minister. It was a mark of his modest surprise that he gave his auto-biography the title *As it Happened*. It was in fact a remarkable series of political accidents that brought him to the leadership. The crisis of 1931 which carried Ramsay Macdonald back to power as head of a so-called National Government almost obliterated the Labour Party. A few stalwarts threw in their lot with Macdonald, a very large number lost their seats, and George Lansbury found himself the leader of a small group in Parliament. That high-minded ineffectual did not last long and the prize, if prize it was, fell into Attlee's lap in 1935 and he became the official leader of the Opposition facing the apparently monolithic battalions in front of and all round him. But when the Labour Party regained something like its proper representation Attlee did not relax his grip and showed no disposition whatever to give place to more experienced Parliamentarians, better administrators, and more popular public figures than he, either then or after the war. He was there, and there he stuck, with a fearless tenacity which he continued to exhibit for the rest of his political life. He must have enjoyed

39

the power and position; he must have felt, like all other Prime Ministers, that nobody else could do the job as well as he; but he gave little or no sign of the enjoyment and his exercise of power often seemed fumbling and nerveless. But he was in his own way as dedicated as Churchill. His whole life and work had been devoted to social reform and his electoral triumph in 1945 gave him opportunities he had scarcely dreamed of. He was, moreover, a strongly patriotic man, aggressively British in his innermost feelings. He loved the army and his service in an infantry regiment in Gallipoli and France in the First World War had left him with a firm faith in the regimental way of doing things. A Government, he felt, should be run in the same way, a strict chain of command, unquestioning obedience, courage, endurance, and conformity with an established code of decent behaviour; and this was in fact very much the way he sought to run his Cabinet. He was irritable, waspish and severe, demanding high standards, and he rarely consulted his colleagues privately. He was the rather irascible Commanding Officer, aloof and alone. But I always felt, as I have written of him before, that he wanted to be more clubbable and convivial than he knew how. This is no more than a hunch on my part and it may be quite wrong, but I fancy he liked the House of Commons, thought of it as a kind of glorified Haileybury, with prefects and house prefects, and new boys, and non-conformist cads and louts whom you snubbed and shunned, strict codes of behaviour and good form, sacred conventions, while its rows and storms and divisions were a series of house matches of no great significance if the school itself were sound. When his second Administration was existing from day to day on a very slender majority, meetings of the Cabinet often took place in the Prime Minister's room in the House of Commons to ensure that Ministers did not miss divisions. The meetings were subject to violent interruption by the imperious ringing of the division bell. On one such occasion, as Attlee and the other Ministers trooped back from the division, he spat out at me, 'Pipped by one'. 'What will you do, Sir?' I anxiously enquired. 'Nothing,' he said, 'I would have done the same to them.' It was a sort of game. A try had been scored against him, but that was not the end of the game. I must confess, however, that I would far rather go to Twickenham than watch Wilson versus Heath from the Strangers' Gallery!

To my mind Eden is a tragic character, though I doubt if he would thank me for saying so. Born into the so-called ruling class, blessed with good brains and good looks, educated at what are still regarded as the very best centres of education, Eton and Christ Church, a brave novitiate in the First World War, followed by a first-class degree, enough money to make a career in politics and the world at his feet. I should guess that he was at first led onwards and upwards in politics less by ambition for power than by a natural instinct that this was his life, that the world of politics and more particularly international politics was the world in which he was destined to have his being and for the service of which these brilliant qualities had been showered upon him. Success came early and with it no doubt the adulation of many, which he had been better without. But he served his country with great distinction and there were few places in the world where his good looks and smart clothes (and special black Homburg hat) did not attract the admiring stare of the populace and where his easy command of his subject did not win applause and respect for the voice of Britain. The quarrels with Chamberlain and the resignation did nothing, in the opinion of most of us, to detract from the importance and the brilliance of this magnetic figure. A Foreign Secretary during a war, in which all the great Powers are involved, has less opportunity to make a special mark than a peace-time Foreign Secretary; but the public knew, and were glad, that when Churchill was taking decisions that affected the destinies of nations and was travelling around the world on missions of imperial splendour, Eden was usually with him, at his side with calm and measured professional advice. I suppose that if politicians did not love power so much, Churchill might have regarded the successful conclusion of the war as the crowning achievement of his stupendous career and accepted all the honours which the Sovereign, acting as usual with the undoubted accord of the people, was eager to bestow on him, leaving the succession to Eden. I do not think that Eden, or any other Conservative politician, could have won the General Election of 1945, but if at that moment Eden, at the age of 48, had become Leader of the Opposition, obliged, as Churchill said, 'to give directions over the whole scene' to his followers

41

in Parliament, to devote his great talents and comprehension to problems other than the Middle East, to magnify his observation of domestic problems, to feel that at any moment the pendulum would swing and that he, without question, would reign supreme in Downing Street, if all that had happened, he might have made a better peace-time Prime Minister than any in this century, except Asquith and Macmillan. But it did not happen, and for the next ten years he continued in opposition and in office, to be, first and foremost, the proposer of foreign policy, and secondly, the heir apparent to an old beech tree, whose heavy shade stunted all growth. There was no doubt that the old beech tree loved Eden the best of all those who gathered in his shade, reckoned him as without any question his successor. But, during Churchill's second administration, Eden was kept at his international last and even in that familiar role he was not neglected by the overriding satrap who still felt that he knew better than any of his subordinates. I have witnessed uncomfortable scenes, scenes at which the Prime Minister assumed so much superiority of touch and poured out so much critical scorn that his Foreign Secretary was affronted and angry and not easily restrained from sweeping out of the room and leaving his resignation behind him. And so the uneasy partnership went on, years of hope unfulfilled piling up on Eden's back and Winston's grip weakened every day but never relaxed. When at last the change came, I suspect that Eden felt in a hurry to make his number, to prove that those long outdated prophecies of the highest achievement were not misconceived, to fulfil the rosy promise which had begun to fade into 'the sere and yellow leaf'. In what field could he attain the champion's prize more easily, and more justifiably, than on his own familiar track? The situation in the Middle East was impossible, Nasser was a potential Hitler, the peace and safety of the whole world depended upon his immediate elimination; here is the chance and here am I, the giant-killer so long denied my prey. This is an over-simplification, of course, and not for one moment do I underestimate the complexity of the political factors, the arguments this way and that. I know far too much about similar situations to be scornfully superficial in my judgment. I am trying to assess the personal stresses and strains which led Eden into what proved to be his tragic descent to Avernus—the thrill of a dark conspiracy, the hasty preparations, the secrecy, the risk, the personal directions and command. Had he not seen it many times before? Had he not seen the old man going through all these stages of bossy interference, reproof and reproach, abuse even, and anger? He could do it just as well; but he did not know, as the old man only just knew, when to sit remote and calm, like a great Commander-in-Chief, surveying the whole scene and bringing his weight of decision into play only when and where it was needed. He had not realised that you cannot command fleets and armies and air forces by telephone from the Cabinet room at 10 Downing Street.

I know nothing of these matters at first hand. I was working in a rather attractive suburb of the great Government Metropolis—the University Grants Committee—and never once during Eden's premiership did I enter the Cabinet Office or No. 10. Moreover I knew well enough, as all civil servants should know, that in times of grave crisis and distress you do not ask for news or information from those friends of yours who happen at that time to be at the nerve centre. I am guessing then, making my own deductions from the various publications, discreet and indiscreet, which followed, and still follow, the event, and I come back to my first thought. If pity and terror, as Aristotle would have it, are the true elements of tragedy, then Eden is a tragic character. After long years of patience he achieved the power, not so much which he craved, but which he had been led to expect. He failed, failed utterly, misled, I fancy, by some friends too ready to flatter, thinking it a mark of courage and resolution to shut his ears to wise and measured advice, seduced into an ungovernable rashness by a deep-seated vanity and suddenly deprived of the essential support of physical health. His name will be for ever synonymous with Suez and however much one can argue that he was right, or nearly right, that a touch, this way or that, would have brought success, the fact is, and will remain, that Suez was a terrible failure. Eden is too proud and too strong to want our pity, but I do not think that any man of my age could look back over the years of promise, when we had a splendid young Englishman speaking for us throughout the world, and not feel pity for the pathetic anti-climax. It has something in common with the Abdication.

What looked like the wreck of a Government and the ruins

43

of a party were turned into a triumph by Harold Macmillan. By care and wisdom, by foresight and an invincible determination not to be scared or pushed around, he had in two years from Suez put his party into an impregnable position, repaired Anglo-American friendship and made some advance, on his own initiative, in the direction of an East/West détente. He was Super Mac and Wonder Mac and at the height of his career the most trusted and most popular peace-time Prime Minister of this century. He had all his life been devoted to the cause of social reform. He knew the desperate evils of widespread unemployment at first hand and he was early in the field with proposals for a mixed economy. He was a rebel in the Tory camp in the 1930's on almost all matters of high policy. He was disgusted by the smug inertia of the Government towards the distressed areas and he abhorred the policy of appeasement and the shame of Munich. No doubt he would have liked power to put his policies into practice, but he made no ingratiating attempts to be given office. This robust independence of spirit is not forgotten by the thoughtful voter; and the common voter moreover likes his political leaders to have a bit of style. I think I can understand why a man like Hugh Gaitskell, utterly sincere himself, a little cold perhaps and rather high-minded, found it impossible to believe in the sincerity of a man who so often adopted a pose of vague indifference or even levity. But the public like that sort of thing and I have described elsewhere how even those tough and forthright New Zealanders felt the magnetism of that offhand manner and that vague stare. He was an actor, no doubt, but he was a very good actor and what is more important he had written his own play. He knew what he wanted to achieve and he knew—at any rate at first—which actors to put in which parts; and I am sure he loved, like all the other Prime Ministers I have discussed, the power to get on with it. It could be argued that the first years of success gave him too much self-confidence and that his unusually severe slaughter of ministerial colleagues in 1962 had the effect of cutting him off from public opinion in his own party and led imperceptibly to the wretched Profumo affair. He found it difficult, again like most Prime Ministers, to bow himself out and just when he had made up his mind to go on leading his party through the next General

Election, his physical condition ruled otherwise and he found himself advising his Sovereign on the choice of a successor from his sickbed in Sister Agnes' Nursing Home.

Now he is writing his own memoirs and writing them— as one would expect—exceedingly well. He is a scholar and a man of taste and in spite of his finesse as a party manager and his outstanding political ability he seems in many respects less like a politician than any other Prime Minister of this century. For me and for many of my friends his compelling charm is that he can feel sensitively, probe deeply and act boldly without ever lapsing into a mood of self-conscious earnestness and unsmiling seriousness. The strange untoward thought obtrudes and he must give it humorous expression. It is this habit which, I think, alienated Gaitskell, but I find solace in it. Some of the roughness of life can be smoothed away by the chance impromptu jest. I heard him speak not long since when he was opening two new boarding houses at St Edward's School, Oxford. His speech was excellent, carefully studied, delivered with his individual charm. A serious passage on the progress of secondary education included something like this : 'The Victorians had great faith in education. They believed that education would make us all good—not as good as Prince Albert of course—but still, good.' To my way of thinking that is worth all the vulgarisms which sometimes escaped his lips— 'There ain't gonna be no war' and 'You've never had it so good'—though these had their political importance too. But his appearance on that ceremonial occasion in Oxford, when he looked very fine and very splendid in his Chancellor's robes, seemed to me less characteristic than a chance meeting in Bond Street one evening quite recently, at about 6.30 p.m. He was dark-suited, hatless, his white hair carefully arranged, his eye glancing up along the street. The rush hour was over and many empty taxis came past this hesitating figure. 'Can I help you?' I asked as I came up with him. 'Oh yes—how kind, how nice to see you'—a limp handshake—'No, no, I just want to go to Victoria Station.' 'There are plenty of taxis,' I said. No, he did not want that; was there a bus? 'Yes,' I said. 'If you stand in this queue a No. 25 will come along' and come along it did, and there he sat on the side bench near the door, his hands resting on a rolled silk umbrella, his fine head tilted upwards, his eyes seemingly unaware of the interested glances of his fellow-passengers. Had he ever been in a London bus before, I wondered as I walked away, pondering upon the eccentric greatness of this lovable man.

Chapter II

THE PUBLIC SERVANT

It is just over a hundred years since the recommendations in the Trevelyan/Northcote report on the reform of the Civil Service began to be effective and in that hundred years the complexities of Government business and the responsibilities of Government have been increased beyond all recognition. In the study of the political history of the eighteenth century and the first sixty or seventy years of the nineteenth it is impossible not to get the impression that a large part of the Prime Minister's and other Ministers' time was taken up in the disposal of patronage, the giving of jobs in Government service to the friends and relations of men whose loyalty Ministers were obliged somehow to retain. Greville, for example, speaks of some Minister 'who made the patronage of the Admiralty instrumental to governing Scotland'. This system of patronage was rife and, although it had the effect no doubt of putting some very able men into important executive posts, it did not produce an effective or industrious Civil Service. This was not of such serious significance while Government accepted responsibility for only a few of the nation's activities—foreign affairs, defence, and, rather reluctantly, the rule of Colonial possessions, and the raising of revenue to pay for these, and a broad economic policy which would go a little way to supporting the rapidly increasing population and the expansion of industry. But as the nineteenth century went on, the social conscience of Governments grew more tender and in any case it became necessary, in order to avoid discontent, famine and tumult, to pay more attention to the needs of all classes of society in a rapidly expanding state. Things could not safely be left to follow their natural course and Government became more and more heavily involved in social services and legislation for them. Whether patronage was good or bad, the system could no longer produce enough competent men to provide Ministers with the much larger and more able staffs which their responsibilities now required. Some other system must be adopted. Moreover the Victorian sense of rectitude was opposed to patronage on such a scale. It was, then, as a result of practical necessity and moral principle that from about 1870 till the present time the normal method of entry into the permanent posts in the Civil Service has been by competitive examination. Now the responsibilities of Government have extended even further and in recent years the demands for more and more well-qualified civil servants have become so insistent and so urgent that I have heard men express doubts about the ability of the system of competitive examination to cope fast enough with a very pressing problem. I am quite sure that the present First Civil Service Commissioner will find a solution to this problem without any recourse to the old system of patronage.

Throughout the period of time covered in my last chapter, all those Prime Ministers and Ministers whom I discussed were served and advised by men of outstanding ability, selected by competitive examination, and accustomed as a result of their training and experience to offer well-informed advice of great objectivity to any Ministers who happened to be in power, well-drilled moreover to carry into effect the final decisions of Ministers or Parliament, whether in accordance with or clean contrary to the advice they had given. It could, I suppose, be argued that with the growth of a Civil Service of first-class quality the job of Ministers has grown easier, and certainly the history of the early part of the nineteenth century leaves one with the impression that Ministers were often short of advice and often obliged to do their own devilling and their own drafting. This has not been the case during this century, but it would be unwise to deduce from this that a Minister's task is any easier. It is easier in one respect—less hard intellectual slogging on his own; but it is more difficult in another— an enormous expenditure of nervous energy and intellectual skill in trying to convince his very clever and very experienced advisers that he is right and they are wrong. He must often pine for the days a hundred years back when a Minister could safely ignore any puny advice submitted to him, especially as his adviser was also his protégé. But these considerations leave no doubt at all that civil servants—I am speaking of the élite, the so-called Administrative Class—have a great deal of power and in the context of this book I want to ask how they acquire it, how they use it and what sort of people they are.

I doubt very much if young men at the universities are attracted into the Administrative Class of the Home Civil Service by the expectation that they will exert power and influence in the nation's affairs. Anyone who has sat on selection boards in competitions for this class knows that one of the most unrewarding questions which can be put to a candidate is 'What attracts you to the Administrative Class?' The candidate, who is after all only 21 or 22, does not often get much further than vague references to interesting work near the centre of things, working with other men of the same kind, doing things—shyly spoken in self-deprecating tones—for the public good and not for profit, a very constant theme this which disturbs industry in its recruitment campaigns. I suppose if a candidate said boldly in answer to this inevitable question, 'because I thirst for power', the selection board would get a very severe shock and the active and retired civil servants on the board would be forced to begin a silent self-inquisition into their own motives and their own practice. I remember asking one of the finest civil servants of my time why he had entered the Administrative Class and he was very frank in his reply. He had been told, he said, that if he got a First in Greats he would be elected to a Fellowship at his College and he would then have spent his life in those delightful fields where work and pleasure to many men are indistinguishable from each other. But by some aberration of the examiners he got a Second and then felt he must look elsewhere. In this uncertain frame of mind, kicking his heels, as all of us have often done, in the College Lodge, he observed a notice inviting applications for a competition for the Administrative Class. That very day was the closing date, and off he rushed to the Appointments Board, filled in a form, sent it off, and in due course sat for the examination, came out third in the list of successes and after years of unremitting toil and absolute devotion became Lord Normanbrook.

Norman Brook was in fact the outstanding civil servant amongst my contemporaries. Edward Bridges, whom some would rate higher, was quite a few years older; but both of them would have disdained the idea that there was a sort of competition amongst civil servants to see who could turn out

49

the most famous. That is not at all the way in which civil servants go to work. The methods and the personality of Norman Brook will illustrate in some respects the aims and ambitions of civil servants, the kind of work they are called upon to do, the way they set about it and the daily life which most of them lead. It is clear from what I have already said that Brook was nursing no insatiable ambition when he roused himself from the habitual indolence of Lodge-lounging and rushed off to make the first mark in the long track of his career. He probably knew almost nothing about the work of the Administrative Class; he just knew that some of his cleverer friends were going in for it and that it seemed an honourable and interesting sort of job. I have no doubt that, unlike some young men today, he took pains to know a little more about it before he appeared for interview before the Civil Service Commissioners. At any rate he scored highly at that interview and also notched up an outstanding mark for moral philosophy, a subject which many men in these days would regard as a perfectly useless foundation for a career in the Civil Service. But the study of moral philosophy may well give a critical balance to mind and temperament and this Brook had in abundance. He started life in the Home Office, generally regarded as an old-fashioned Department, that is to say a Department in which traditional methods of work and certain conventions of behaviour are thought to be important. Certainly throughout his career Brook was a master of order and precision and insisted on it in others, and something of this, I dare say, was due to his Home Office training. His intellectual power was of the first order, his mental and physical stamina remarkable, and above all he cultivated an equability and a calmness of judgment which gave confidence to all above and below him in the many and constant times of crisis which occur at the centre of the political whirlpool. One of his admiring colleagues endowed him with divine attributes—'unresting, unhasting', he called him and no better definition could be found. He was the exact opposite of a certain type of higher civil servant not wholly unknown—the sort of man who allows himself to get as highly charged as the load of work he is handling. He feels that as the work is urgent his whole style and manner must be urgent too. He must move quickly, darting from his room, slamming the door, running noisily and awkwardly along the passages. He must demand the instant production of documents, which he hardly needs, he must surround himself with files and reports and complain that the one he really wants is not there. He must give his instructions and dictate his letters and minutes in jumbled tones of incoherent agitation. He does not make life easy for those around him and the work, which Brook would do impeccably with perfect composure in one hour, will take him three.

I knew Brook first in the last months of the war and then from 1950 to 1954 I served under him in the Cabinet Office. A closer and happier collaboration could not have been possible. It ripened with each year and in the last year before I went to Kenya in April, 1954, any misgiving or misunderstanding between us was out of the question. His standards in everything were very high. Careless work excited his contempt and even a kind of icy anger, but I never saw him lose his temper, however much he was provoked from whatever quarter, whether by the ineptitude of colleagues and subordinates or by unreasonable Ministerial exactions from above. He remained outwardly unruffled, as unruffled as his habitually neat clothes. He dressed for the office immaculately, as Londoners used to dress between the wars, the short black coat and striped trousers very often, and never anything gayer than a well-cut subfusc suit. He did not, however, insist upon uniformity of dress for all the Cabinet Office staff, but wide deviations made him uncomfortable. When I turned up one Monday morning from a country week-end in some sort of check tweed suit, he instantly expressed the hope—it was almost a command—that I was not going to attend the Cabinet Meeting looking like that. He viewed with some dismay, but in a spirit of reluctant toleration, the increasing tendency, amongst a succession of devoted private secretaries, towards a careless disorder in the dress and a dislike for hats of any kind. These are not trivialities, but manifestations of something very deep and very powerful within him, a craving almost, for order and neatness and balance. It was apparent in his temper, it was apparent in his clothes and it was apparent in his work.

I know nothing of the work of the Secretary of the Cabinet and his staff at the present time. That it has changed since the

1950's, of which I am writing, can be deduced from the present size and grading of the staff. But I daresay it still remains true that the Secretary of the Cabinet is responsible for very complex and very important articulating machinery. Everything of significance in Government transactions must go to Cabinet Committees and finally to the Cabinet itself. The handling of these vital matters, the arrangements for preliminary consultation and discussion, whether in this Committee or in that, the decision to submit them to the Cabinet itself and the manner in which they should be submitted—all these are questions on which the advice of the Secretary of the Cabinet and his staff is indispensable. Each Ministry of course knows its own affairs better than the Cabinet Office. It knows that it wants to get Cabinet approval for a particular measure, say for the building of a large number of new primary schools, and it knows that it must have some sort of preliminary acquiescence, if not approval, from the Treasury. It does not know—it is not its business to know—how many other Ministers have equally urgent projects, demanding, not necessarily money, but Parliamentary time, and more acceptable perhaps in terms of Government policy. The Cabinet Secretariat knows all this and knows how to get the questions thrashed out and when and in what form to advise Ministers to submit their proposals to the Cabinet. The Secretary of the Cabinet knows best of all. His advice on matters of this kind is sought, not only by the top civil servants in different Ministries, but by the Ministers themselves. How can we make progress, how can we get our way? If the response is cool and damping, the Secretary of the Cabinet may find himself belaboured and besieged, incessantly nagged. But he has other considerations in his mind. He knows what the Prime Minister thinks and what the Prime Minister wants or will not consider. He is the Prime Minister's closest adviser. The Prime Minister has no executive Department to administer, no divisions or corps to command. He is the Supreme Commander and the Secretary of the Cabinet is his Chief of Staff. If this is not a position of power, I do not know what it is; but Brook, I am sure, never thought of it in these terms. The course of his career had brought him to that position and he found there was a big job to do; so he did it, for many years, in a big way. The better you do a job of this kind—the job, as it were, of a universal joint—the more insistent the job becomes. The more you gain the confidence of Ministers and senior civil servants and of the Prime Minister himself, the more frequent the inroads upon your time and nervous energy. The greater your reputation for a wise and balanced judgment, the more your advice is sought and relied upon, and once you feel you have inspired this trust in yourself, the harder you strive to deserve it. It is the kind of job moreover where delegation is almost impossible. If the Minister cannot speak to Brook he will not speak to anyone; the most useful thing the subordinates can do is to create the same deep confidence and trust on their level, not to hope to be a stand-in for the master.

Brook knew all of this, of course, though he had no time to analyse it in this sort of way. He must equally have known that he held in his hands a great deal of power. He had not courted it but there it was. I do not say he was upset or disappointed, let alone dismayed, by what had happened to him, but his reaction was quite different from the politician's. He did not feel that now at last he had the power to put his ideas into practice. What he felt was that he must exercise this power in such a way as to bring about the most orderly and rapid transaction of Government business. That was all. That is the civil servant's duty, but a great deal of influence is comprehended in that duty. I remember that when I was joined in the Cabinet Office by a young Assistant Secretary, hand-picked and carefully selected, I was at pains to explain to him that, although it was the duty of members of the Cabinet Secretariat to brief the Chairmen of their Cabinet Committees, the brief was a procedural brief only and it was no part of their job to criticise the substance of a Department's proposals. Obviously the Department knew far more about the subject than they did. This ambitious young man looked a little crest-fallen at my avuncular admonishments. But when I showed him copies of briefs which I had submitted to the Chairmen of my Committees and which Brook had submitted to the Prime Minister, he was quick to see that 'procedure' has wide frontiers and that advice on procedure can do a lot to further or to hamper a project and even to frustrate it altogether. It may well be that the Secretary knows that some contrary or

53

complementary project is being hatched in some other Department and that the effective conduct of public business requires haste or delay or whatever it may be. The Chairman must be warned of this, and he must be warned of the objections any project is likely to meet from other members of the Committee and advised how these objections might be overcome. The Chairman—Prime Minister or any other Chairman—need not accept the advice, but there is no doubt at all that, if the Secretary deserves confidence and attention, his voice is persistently powerful. And Brook had acquired the confidence and attention not only of successive Prime Ministers but of other Ministers and senior civil servants as well.

He had acquired them by unremitting toil and devotion to duty over many years, but there was a very human side to him too. Brook was tall and distinguished-looking, very fair, very blue-eyed—much more a Saxon than a Norman—and by inclination convivial, liking the company of other men, liking sport, and glorying in the successes of Oxford, particularly on the river, enjoying his golf at Woking and cultivating, as the years went by, a fastidious taste in wine. On the other hand he was in some ways a shy, even a timid, man and he did not find it easy to make his way with strangers or to relax in mixed company which was not familiar to him. At home and among his friends he could be gay and full of laughter, ready to joke about the pompous situations in which we had found ourselves all day, to take lightly and humorously the critical vexations which had tormented us from hour to hour.

Cabinet Office Secretaries spend, or should spend, much of their working lives in silence, listening with deep concentration to the disputes and arguments in their Committees and pondering upon the most constructive way of formulating the minutes and making sure that positive action will follow. As Brook and I emerged from No. 10 after listening in attentive silence to two and a half hours of close and difficult argument in Cabinet, his tongue would be liberated and an incessant and striking monologue would keep pace with us as we walked across Downing Street, through the Foreign Office courtyard, across King Charles Street, into the new Public Offices and along the mazelike passages back to his office. There were hours of strenuous thinking and more listening ahead of us, until perhaps we snatched half-an-hour together at about 7 p.m. for a drink in the mess. But that was very rarely the end of his working day. Once I remember he had planned a very special party for his Silver Wedding. He was to leave the office at about 6 p.m.—a very early night for him—climb into a tail coat and white tie and for once in a blue moon spend a festive and untroubled evening with his wife and his friends. No urgent business was likely to turn up, he thought, but would I mind holding the fort in case some unexpected emergency arose? He had not been gone an hour, before my telephone rang and the Prime Minister, then Mr Attlee, instructed me to call a meeting of the Cabinet forthwith to take place in his room in the House of Commons at 8.30 p.m. that evening. It was very urgent, he said, and rang off. I set the wheels in violent motion, immediate telephone calls to Ministers to attend, rapid preparation of documents, hasty arrangements in the Prime Minister's room and so on. As a matter of duty I telephoned Brook, begging him not to disturb his evening, assuring him that I could cope. But his sense of responsibility prevailed. The meeting started without him. I had duly explained his absence to the Prime Minister, who made no comment, but after about ten minutes the door was pushed open and in he came, a well-starched, resplendent figure, and took his seat beside the Prime Minister. Sir Charles Barry, I thought, who had designed these gothic extravaganzas, had had in his mind as the denizens of these inappropriate and inconvenient apartments men dressed up in grandeur like Brook, rather than the drab Cabinet Ministers who sat around the table in their well-worn workaday clothes. If it was perhaps the only occasion on which the Secretary of the Cabinet appeared at a meeting in white tie and tails it was certainly one of the few meetings at which Cabinet Ministers—led on this occasion by the vulgar exuberance of Hugh Dalton—banged the table and shouted 'Hear, Hear.' In this mood of unprecedented enthusiasm the meeting broke up and Brook, after giving me the necessary instructions, went back to his interrupted gaieties.

Attlee, if I remember rightly, spent the next few days ordering preparations for his rush visit to Washington to try to persuade President Truman to curtail the Korean war; and

Brook and I, and many others, feverishly prepared the briefs, the information, the advice which he would need for this confrontation. One very cold and snowy Sunday afternoon Brook and I laboured at No. 10 with the economic and financial questions which the Americans would expect him to answer. We became confused and uncertain with subjects not intimately known to us but a telephone call soon brought a high Treasury official from the Sunday warmth and relaxation of his home to our rescue. That is what civil servants are like, and it is because they are like that and because for the most part they use their power in the service of Ministers and not for their own ends, that Attlee, I have no doubt, spent that cold Sunday afternoon on his own personal affairs or even having a rest before his midnight flight. He had perfect confidence that he would be given all the briefs he needed and he quite rightly left us to get on with it.

The British Civil Service, though now increasingly criticised, still comes in for a good deal of praise from many quarters at home and abroad—incorruptible, objective, dutiful, self-effacing, industrious, of unquestioned integrity and high intellectual ability, and so on, enough to turn the heads of the most modest men. Yet arrogance is not a common feature of this remote and gifted class. From time to time one or two will succumb to the temptation of a contemptuous cock-sureness, a confident certainty that the Minister is no more than a puppet controlled by the experienced and deft manipulations of his Civil Service advisers. When this happens nemesis is not slow. Ill-considered comments casually overheard and reported soon bring retribution. A more common temptation is to a sort of smug inaction, a self-satisfied lethargy. After all many of the qualities for which the higher Civil Service is praised are somewhat negative and it is easier to retain this honourable reputation if risks are not taken, if mistakes are not made. The glittering promise of young men, entering the Administrative Class, is not infrequently extinguished by a blanket of timid leadership from above, powerful only to deplore zeal and to mistrust audacious ideas. 'We are very clever men, we do not make mistakes, we must not mislead,' they seem to be saying to each other. The spectre of a mutual admiration society is always within haunting distance, anxious to put its unwholesome spell upon these insulated men, to turn their disputes into inconclusive competitions in cleverness, encompassing them in an accursed circle of obstacles and objections so that the springs of spontaneous enthusiasm are dried up, and, even if no absolute objection can be found to a proposed course of action, agreement and approval never go beyond 'I do not dissent from this view'—each non-dissenter wishing to escape disgrace and derision if some non-non-dissenter succeeds in finding a flaw in the proposal so far overlooked. The really top-class civil servants steer clear of these absurdities and it is their distinguishing mark that their mental processes do not come to a lame full stop before the obstinate mound of objections which they have raised, but go on questing and probing for circumventing or surmounting paths. I have made this clear by reference to Brook's work and attitude as Secretary of the Cabinet. It is equally true of the Permanent Secretaries, the official heads of the great Departments of State. Most of those I have known were men and women of great quality who saw quite clearly that their duty was not only to save their Minister from mistakes but to help him to success. I can still recall with something like awe meetings of committees composed almost exclusively of Permanent Secretaries of which I was secretary. Not much was said but what was said was weighty, crisp, effective, each member sure of his part and certain of his aim. When I think of these occasions now I am reminded of a remark of President Kennedy. He had assembled for dinner at the White House the Western Hemisphere Nobel prizewinners and he welcomed them as 'the most extraordinary collection of talent, of human knowledge, that has ever been gathered together at the White House', and then added, 'with the possible exception of when Thomas Jefferson dined alone.' The collection of talent, the weight of intellect, was there in Conference Room A in the Cabinet Office, but I cannot think of a civil servant, sitting there alone, who could have matched Thomas Jefferson. It would have needed a Macaulay at least.

I have already touched upon the work of these Permanent Secretaries, the official heads of the great Departments of State, their responsibility for advising Ministers, for making sure that Ministers know the pitfalls in front of their eager footsteps, understand what is realistic, what can be done and what cannot, and never act with a rash indifference to consequences. How far will the farmers press their opposition? What effect would a rise in the price of bread and bacon have upon the economic policies of the Government and above all on the voting propensities of the electorate? Can there be a cut-and-dried national fuel policy and if there is one what effect would this have upon coal mining, upon gas and oil producers and again upon the economy as a whole and upon the passions of the voters? What is the right and realistic policy for railways? Are railways a commercial undertaking or a social service? And deeper and more perplexing questions still—how do we balance our payments without restricting industrial growth and development? How do we curb inflation, put a merciful stop to the diabolical spiral of prices and wages? And testing vexing moral questions too which in these days no Government can turn its back on—should we permit cigarette advertising, should we restrict drugs and if so which drugs and how? There is no end to the problems which confront Governments and no limit to the advice civil servants must be ready to provide— a wide range of advice from moral questions of delicate complexity to homespun opinions on very down-to-earth matters. Nothing ever illustrated this to me more forcibly than a train of questioning which took its unrehearsed way through the interview of a candidate for the Administrative Class. A highly-placed academic, a woman of remarkable quality and achievement, took the candidate up to an elevated level of speculation on theoretical issues, moral and metaphysical questions, designed, quite rightly, to test his powers of abstract thought. The whole thing was well conducted and well answered and when her inquisition was over I handed the questioning to a strongly practical, realistic, positive, constructive civil servant, a great favourite of mine. 'Well,' he began, 'I am sorry to bring you so suddenly down to earth from these philosophic heights; but I have been facing a practical problem for several days and I wondered if you might have a view. It is the sort of thing civil servants are constantly asked to give advice about. There has been a row about a meat pie, the purchaser of the meat pie complaining to the Ministry of Food that after analysis he had found almost no real meat in the pie. Now the question is—do

58

you think the Minister ought to accept any responsibility at all for the amount of meat in a pie, or is it not simply a case of "Caveat Emptor"?'

It is surprising in some ways that these top civil servants can give advice, usually very sound advice, on such a wide variety of topics—surprising because they belong to an élite class and from the age of 22 can, if they so wish, lead a daily life divorced from the life of ordinary men. It is true that this divorce, this insulation, from the common traffic of the world, its arguments, its prejudices, its bargainings, its mistrust, its ignorance, helps them to preserve that calm objective judgment which at the outset of their careers brought them a high mark in moral philosophy. But for the most part these civil servants are not men of the world; they do not know and do not care, or even dare, to know how the world wags. They live in a strange restricted world with narrow frontiers of convention which constrict their daily lives. I have never felt really comfortable about the routine we were offering fifteen years ago to young men joining the Administrative Class, a routine which would vary only with the habits of advancing years. Most of them would still move and have their daily being in a sort of intellectual camp, bounded by the Houses of Parliament, the Embankment as far as Charing Cross, Northumberland Avenue, Trafalgar Square, Pall Mall, St James's Park, Storey's Gate and so back to Parliament Square, a narrow world indeed where the only outsiders were banner-carrying deputations from Jarrow or West Cumberland, carefully and tactfully shepherded by the police, where most of the pubs were clubs, and the only fresh air and the only natural fauna and flora closely encompassed within the confines of St James's Park. This beautiful park, lovingly tended by extravagant gardeners, whose bedding plants would keep a thousand private gardens in constant and uncomplaining bloom, was our lung, our exercise ground in which for a brief half hour in the middle of the day we could cast aside the perplexing problems of the advice we should give to Ministers, the methods we should use to advance public business, in fact forget about how we could most profitably use the power which was without question in our grasp, and enjoy a world in which we certainly had no power at all— a world where tufted ducks and coots fought for a momentary victory, where pelicans swam awkwardly but imperiously, driving lesser birds out of their cumbersome way, a world where the grass, the flowers and the stately plane trees tried to remind us that the true significance of life was not entirely comprehended within the walls of our prosaic offices and conference rooms. If the park was the only outdoor relief from the dusty airless arena of our daily disputations, the clubs were the only indoor relief, those grandiose edifices ranged in forbidding dignity along Pall Mall, up St James's Street and round St James's Square, solid reminders of the affluence of the small upper and upper-middle classes which dominated political and professional life in this country for one hundred and fifty years and more, built without any regard to economy of space, vast entrance halls large enough to house huge country cattle markets and much less useful, spacious smoking rooms with elaborate ceilings almost out of sight and restrictive regulations about membership and good form which make the more conservative and traditional trade unions seem almost liberal and up-to-date. I am writing now of the decade after the war. Things have changed since then. Some of these clubs have brought themselves into line with the social habits and needs of the second half of the twentieth century. Some, it is felt in some quarters, have gone too far. Members, admitted with only the most perfunctory scrutiny, have brought with them habits more suitable to a station hotel. They dump their suitcases and overcoats at random in the public rooms, they hold tough discussions in loud tones with business associates in the usually silent recesses of the library, they can be heard in the bar, ordering 'Similar, Miss, please', they read books at dinner and blow smoke all over the breakfast table—while old Sir George sits rigid by the window in an attitude of pained superiority. Almost all clubs have now admitted women, with proper limiting rules of course, with the not surprising result that women, who for so many years fed their imaginations with pictures of elegant rooms and with lurid conjectures about drink and gambling and bawdy talk, found that the elegance had degenerated into a kind of drab luxury and that the club habits of their husbands were just as sober and dull and timid as their habits at home, the only difference being that in their clubs men talked shop 'without intermission or remorse of voice.' Fifteen years ago women for the most part were confined to a ladies' side where the food and service were usually inferior to those provided on the other side of the safety curtain. And on the other side of the safety curtain members in their much cherished masculine insulation followed a strange way of life.

The days were long since past when these clubs formed the natural meeting places for caballing men anxious to achieve power and place. The Reform Club, built by Barry as a double of the British Embassy in Constantinople, had for many years lent its pretentious wastes of space to concourses of high-minded Liberals. In the decade after the war the Liberals were few and far between both inside and outside the club. There was no more political conspiracy, just a handful of civil servants leaning against the statues of Liberal politicians, now marble ghosts ranged around that vast atrium, and discussing not how to achieve power but how to help Ministers use it wisely. Nothing like the famous Carlton Club meeting in 1922, which brought poor Bonar Law to No. 10, ever happened again; and the war had made senior Generals, Admirals and Air Marshals reluctant to expose themselves to importunate questioning in the Service Clubs. Rich men still preferred White's and a game of backgammon, but neither there nor in Brooks's nor Boodle's were the rash extravagances and absurdities of the Regency to be seen. Some clubs, situated outside the parish of St James's, notably the Garrick and the Savile, retained their special identity, but even so were rather faint reflections of their lively and distinguished past. The fact was that the social habits of the upper-middle classes, which for the most part provided the membership, had changed so completely that, in the evenings at any rate, most clubs were more like museums. A few elderly men, lonely and aimless, hobbled slowly from one room to another. The food was scarce, the heating meagre; and the treasures, collected with such pride over the years, the pictures, the busts, the medals, the animal heads, the rare books, looked undusted and neglected as members passed by them with familiar inattention. Elderly servants, in an astonishing spirit of loyal devotion, strove against the crippling onset of age to retain the high standards of their clubs. There was no-one to replace them.

From time to time I gave a small dinner party in my club

for members of my own staff and one or two others and always the service was good and the chef, if given advance notice, produced as good a meal as could be got in those rather Lenten days; and there was at that time no lack of excellent claret. After dinner we repaired to the billiard room at the top of the house. Apart from my occasional visits the room was generally empty and forlorn. There was no constant heating, the chairs were in rickety disarray and the table in a sort of damp disuse. Warmed by our claret we played light-hearted snooker. From time to time a loyal retainer tottered in with a tray of drinks fetched from a distant source and carried with slow and measured care to the chill of our upper room. All the members, except for us and the residents, were at home assisting with the household chores. There was no longer an evening ticket of leave for the married man.

The scene at lunch was different, more animated, more crowded and less comfortable. Members poured in from their offices in Whitehall, stood in dense groups insisting on their pink gins, queued up for tables in an over-populated and under-staffed coffee room, exchanging opinions on the content of their work in loud and confident tones. Not infrequently there was little left to eat when at last they got a table but the flow of 'shop' continued unabated. By 2.30 the place was dead again. Some resident members retired to the library, a huge, high-ceilinged room with a movable stairway available to fetch down the dusty denizens of the top shelves, and settling themselves in deep red leather chairs, placed a noble book upon the book rest attached to the chair arm, and fell into a stertorous sleep. Others played bridge in a strongly competitive spirit. At about 4.30 the smell of tea and anchovy toast stirred the sleeping bookmen back to life and put an end to the arguments at the bridge table.

The park and the club, it seemed in those days, were almost the only outside world the average civil servant knew. Of course he knew his own home, probably in a London suburb, but his habits of work were so severe that he saw little of it and had no nervous or mental energy left to want to move far outside it in the late evenings or at week-ends. This is not an ambitious way of life but it helps to preserve a narrow integrity. At the higher levels of the Service horizons were wider and negotiations with Commonwealth and foreign countries often required the presence of civil servants from the Treasury, the Board of Trade, the Ministry of Civil Aviation and so on. These civil servants, of course, were not professional experts but members of the élite Administrative Class drawn from the appropriate department. Such delicate negotiations, was the view, could not be handled by professionals with one-track minds and no sensitive comprehension of personalities, no understanding of the lessons of history. This attitude is now much derided, but it was dictated by a worthy principle. Civil servants enjoyed much power, power which in the wrong hands could be wantonly and dangerously used. It was wiser and safer, therefore, to keep it in the hands of this small élite class, which, because of its education, its traditions, its experience and its insulated way of life, could be trusted to be discreet and self-effacing. This was not always a sound judgment but it had much to commend it, and it was good for the civil servants, too, to see a little more of the world. Treasury officials, responsible for what used to be known as overseas finance, found themselves constantly in Washington discussing the convertibility of sterling; senior officials of the Board of Trade travelled about the world making and unmaking commodity agreements and trying to twist the complexities of GATT to our advantage; the organizations created first by the Brussels Treaty and then by the North Atlantic Treaty often attracted visits to the capitals of Western Europe by civilian officials in the Ministry of Defence, and the novel problems of civil aviation soon gave rise to complicated international issues which, in the opinion of members of the Ministry of Civil Aviation, were too difficult and dangerous to leave in the hands of Ambassadors and High Commissioners. It was remarkable, in fact, how ingenious a few alert and enthusiastic civil servants were in finding reasons for swanning around. But it was only a few; for the most part civil servants suffered without protest their restricted surroundings.

Norman Brook, I suppose, became in the end the most travelled civil servant of all time. At the time when it was very uncertain if India would stay in the Commonwealth after independence he was sent on a very sensitive mission to all Commonwealth capitals. This mission, which he performed with the utmost zeal and with great success, left him with a particular affection for the Commonwealth and especially perhaps for Canada. In the last ten or twelve years of his service Prime Ministers rarely travelled without him, because by then his calm steadiness of judgment seemed indispensable in all circumstances. It was not because Brook set himself up as an expert in foreign affairs. No, his power was a tranquillising power, the power to reduce thorny complexities to straight-forward issues, to arrange arguments in lucid order, to steady the boat in what he called 'this somewhat tempestuous world of ours', to remain objective and unruffled amid all the displays of vanity and ill-temper and all the exhibitions of prejudice, ignorance and rash judgment. Whatever the impasse, he could see the next move and advise clearly on the most promising procedure. This was power of a most unusual kind. He took no delight in it, as most men do when they feel that it has fallen to their lot to influence and persuade other men, men moreover in much higher and more conspicuous stations, to plant their footsteps on the right path, not so much to advise what they should say or do, but to suggest the pace and direction of their progress. He never seemed to be excited or elated by all this and he might be indignant or worried at my definitions of his power. He was a very modest man, not diffident about his abilities, not unaware of the repute in which other men held him, but deeply suspicious and timid about public acclaim and prominence, and nervous, even, of exercising any form of dominance over others in the Civil Service or the fighting services.

I can recall an example of this demeanour. The situation arose not so very long after the war when great Commanders had seemed, in the public eye, so much more important than civil servants, and were indeed far more renowned. It had become necessary to have a very thorough and profound review of defence expenditure and to try to make a projection of our likely commitments in the years immediately ahead. The Prime Minister, Winston Churchill, had simply instructed Brook to see that this was done and had made no comment about the method or machinery. Questions of machinery are rather dull anyway, but for various reasons I advised Brook that the method most likely to succeed under the circumstances was to set up a special working party with himself in the chair and a membership composed of the three Chiefs of Staff themselves and equally lofty representatives from the Foreign Office and the Treasury. I was to be secretary, assisted by a colonel, a man of considerable ability, who was on my staff. Brook acknowledged the force of my argument but he was uncertain, hesitant and worried. It was rare, almost unknown, he said, for a civil servant to preside over the Chiefs of Staff. He doubted very much if they would accept the arrangement and in any case he felt fairly sure that the Prime Minister would not like it at all. On the first point I was able to reassure him; my contacts in the world of defence were closer than his and I knew the respect in which the Chiefs held Brook and their willingness at all times to consult him and accept his advice. On the second point he was nearly right. He agreed, at length, to put the proposed machinery to the Prime Minister and to seek his approval. The Prime Minister was surprised and a little disturbed. It was unusual, he said, contrary to traditional practice, for a civilian official to preside over the Chiefs of Staff. Was Sir Norman sure about this? Inwardly, I have no doubt, the Prime Minister welcomed the arrangement because he had more confidence in Sir Norman's judgment than in that of any other official, civil or military. Finally the Prime Minister gave his approval and the machinery was set in motion. No defence review really achieves what its promoters desire, but whatever the shortcomings of the result, there was no grit in the machinery; all worked smoothly and harmoniously.

The reluctant modesty which Brook displayed on this occasion, his general dislike of dominant attitudes and his alarm, almost, at the possibility of being caught in the limelight are characteristic of most higher civil servants. It is their training, their tradition, to efface themselves in public, never to make political speeches or write political articles and to publish nothing unless the subject is as far from their work as the poetry of Humbert Wolfe was from his daily routine in the Ministry of Labour. It is a healthy enough attitude; the Minister takes the kicks, he shall have the ha-pence. But civil servants have up to now received many honours from the Sovereign—far more, it is thought in some quarters, than they deserve—and they are often to be seen looking slightly self-conscious in the chivalrous adornment 'of the invincible knights of old' eating their dinner at the top table of the vast annual gathering of some professional institution in a London hotel; but that is about the limit of their outward display. I used sometimes in a simple spirit of curiosity to ask candidates for the Administrative Class and the Foreign Service whether they could name any Ambassadors or leading civil servants. Never, I think, did any candidate manage to name a civil servant. Ambassadors some candidates could manage, but the Ambassadors of that period were much easier to memorise because of their abnormal Christian names. Esler, Ivone, Gladwyn, Alvary and Pierson stayed in the mind more readily than Frank, Harold, Edward, Archie and Norman. The question was of no importance and carried no marks, but the answers made me wonder if a little more glamour, a little more renown might not be a good recruiting point for the Administrative Class. I soon convinced myself that any relaxation of severe standards in that direction might imperceptibly lead towards a situation in which civil servants began to misuse the great power attached to their office.

If civil servants were modest and retiring in Ministerial and military circles, they were not always so in the course of their work. Brook, as I have said, did not like dominant attitudes, but he could be sharp and severe when the work submitted to him was bad or when, in his judgment, highly-placed colleagues were actuated more by personal vanity than by a sense of public service. But he disliked very much the occasions on which he felt obliged to exhibit, however mildly, irritation or contempt; it was all the more effective for his measured and contained method of reproach. In this he differed from some other civil servants. In the Colonial Office, for example, the relations between some of the permanent civil servants in London and members of the Colonial Service, later to be called the Overseas Civil Service, did not always seem as easy as they might have been. It is, of course, a universal experience for those in the front line, as it were, the active doers, to feel that those in the rear headquarters who are sending out a stream of ridiculous orders know nothing whatever about the realities of the situation. This is a commonplace of war and every Ambassador and High Commissioner has had the same impression from time to time, although he, almost certainly, has himself in the course of his career been the transmitter of these unwelcome and unrealistic instructions and can at least guess at the justification for them. Ambassadors and High Commissioners spend part of their service overseas and part in London, and this alternation of responsibility makes them sensitive and comprehending. The Colonial Office and the Colonial Service organised themselves differently. It was rare for officials in the Colonial Office who were members of the Administrative Class of the Home Civil Service to spend much, if any, time in the Colonial Territories; and even if they went overseas for a year or two they normally worked in the secretariat and not in the field. There was a system by which some selected Colonial Service officials did a two-year stint in London in the Colonial Office. They were known, rather obscurely, as beachcombers. For family reasons they enjoyed their spell at home and learnt as much as they were allowed about the problems of Whitehall. But to an outside observer there did not always seem to be a close mingling and mutual understanding between the Colonial Office and the Colonial Service.

During my spell in the Cabinet Office, from 1950 to 1954, I used from time to time to organise and run a two-day course on defence subjects. The Colonial Office thought it wise to give Colonial Service officials, who worked most of their time within the confines of a single district, province or territory, a wider view of the politico-strategic problems that affected the British Government all over the globe. This was a sensible intention and I organised talks on defence topics, including intelligence, by the accepted Whitehall experts of that time—one of the Vice-Chiefs of Staff for example, and the Chairman of the Joint Intelligence Committee. In consequence the talks were very well-informed, though sometimes, it seemed to me, too much information was administered and the poor Colonial Service officials—who were giving up two days of their precious leave—went back to their homes in the confused discomfort of indigestion. They must have suffered also from another rather uncomfortable sensation. At the end of each talk, in accordance with the normal custom at such conferences, questions were invited from the patient auditors. It is not always easy to ask intelligent questions about subjects little studied and not fully understood. Indeed this must be one of the occupational terrors of royalty. The poor Colonial Service officials at my conferences found themselves not infrequently squashed flat by the stinging retorts delivered *de haut en bas* by the members of the Colonial Office who flanked me at the top table. I wonder if it was a kind of jealousy which made the Colonial Office so eager to exhibit their superior powers. After all a civil servant sitting in Whitehall, devising instructions for Colonial Governors, does not have anything like the same sense of direct power as any District Commissioner in the remotest confines of Empire, who finds himself personally responsible each hour of each day for the health, welfare and good behaviour of his numerous unlettered subjects and for the direct administration of law and order. That is real power, power with a more immediate impact than that exercised by any other public servant. Whatever the political quarrels and misgivings and dissensions that have attended the valiant effort to transform an Empire into a Commonwealth, I do not believe that any responsible citizen of any ex-Colonial territory, speaking from his heart, would hesitate to pay a deep tribute of respect—and indeed of affection—to the men who exercised this power and to the 'system' which produced them. No Colonial Governor ever enjoyed such unfettered power as his own District Commissioners. At his level he was tethered by a political rope at which the Secretary of State, reacting to insistent pressure, was continually tugging. When I was in Kenya in 1954, in the midst of the Mau Mau rebellion, I was surprised and impressed by the strong political sense of the Governor and his most senior advisers, who submitted issues to the decision of the Secretary of State, when I should have rashly blundered on.

It has been said that the public schools were specially devised to produce Empire-builders, the unselfish upholders of the white man's burden, and that now that we have no Empire there is no longer any need for public schools. That argument has no place in this chapter. But if the public schools produced empire-builders they also produce British Ambassadors. My experience has taught me that young men of ability are very much attracted by a career in the Foreign, now the Diplomatic,

Service. It seems much more romantic and glamorous than that of a member of the Administrative Class. Romantic and glamorous it may be, but I doubt if it is more influential, except in those alternate periods when a diplomat is serving at home and advising the Foreign Secretary. In such circumstances his function is very like that of his opposite number in the Home Civil Service. When he is abroad his power, or influence, is much less direct, much more subtle and hard to identify. The career of a diplomat, his functions, powers and responsibilities, has changed fundamentally in the last hundred years. The speed of communications alone has curtailed his discretion. In any corner of the earth the all-pervasive Foreign Secretary can speak to him on the telephone, or, when things look really black or attractively bright, jump into an aeroplane himself and take the leading part in some jubilation or some critical negotiation, which a hundred and fifty years ago the Ambassador would have conducted in imperial splendour, in the comfortable knowledge that no further instructions could reach him for weeks. This was power indeed, and power which had to backed by a fine discretionary sense and a very cool nerve. There are moments still when this power can be exercised, when these superior qualities have to be brought into play, but for the most part an Ambassador, or High Commissioner, acts upon instructions very promptly and very expeditiously received. They arrive at inconvenient times, despatched from London in frenzied haste just as the treasured day off or week-end is about to begin, and often received at a moment when Her Majesty's plenipotentiary is perhaps playing a round of golf with a somewhat anti-British politician whom he wishes to charm, or taking a rest between an over-elaborate curry lunch and an evening party offered by himself to a Diplomatic Corps, detached, critical and boring, who have all been to this sort of party before.

It is, however, quite wrong to argue that because of rapid communications and an omnipresent Foreign Secretary, the Diplomatic Service might just as well be wound up or at any rate reduced to the status of an information and postal service. The British Ambassador or High Commissioner lives out his daily life amongst the citizens of another nation. To most of them he does in fact represent his country. His appearance, his manners, his behaviour, his speeches, add up to their image of what is meant by British. This is a very heavy daily responsibility, in which his wife has a most significant share. They cannot discharge this responsibility by putting on fine clothes and striking lordly attitudes at parties, so generously given by foreign Missions to each other on every possible occasion. The impression made at these extravagant and artificial entertainments is of little account. What matters is to create bonds of natural friendship and understanding with the nationals of the country in which they are serving, to make them feel respect, affection, trust for Britain and the British. The sudden arrival of a harassed and overwrought Foreign Secretary at an hour of crisis has no contribution to make to this particular function. He will be closeted for hours of tough dispute with his opposite numbers and if he makes any public appearance at all he is likely to be too tired and anxious to be able to put over his natural charm and humanity, or so determined to throw care aside that he suddenly behaves like a mountebank.

In his daily routine the Ambassador makes contacts with Ministers and officials. He may not have any startling message to deliver, no sharp confrontation, no allurements in the direction of an early détente; all the better. It is in these daily contacts, the friendly exchange of views, that he establishes the understanding and sympathy which are essential in times of stress.

It is almost impossible, I am told, to create this atmosphere in iron curtain countries. I find this easy to believe considering how rarely it is achieved in countries where natural affinities are strong; but where it is achieved its value is rare and precious. Field-Marshal Sir John Dill was not an Ambassador in name, but in fact the daily influence of his gentle and impressive personality upon General George Marshall was one of the biggest factors in bringing about the Anglo-American unity which won the war. I imagine, though I do not know it at first hand, that Lord Harlech played a similar role in establishing such a close relationship between President Kennedy and Mr Macmillan.

It must have been hard, after the return of de Gaulle to power, for ambassadors to foster and expand the warm feelings of friendship which many Englishmen and Frenchmen have for each other. The last Ambassador, Sir Patrick Reilly, was a highly skilled professional, a man of natural good taste and friendly nature. So was his predecessor, Sir Pierson Dixon, universally beloved, a man in whom the wisdom of restraint and the limitless power of patience were manifest. Lord Gladwyn was a different type, devoted to the European cause, realistic, pungent, astringent, a notable personality, whom nobody, not even de Gaulle, could ignore, a man who, when he represented us on the Security Council in New York, attracted the eyes and ears of the world, eager to tune in and watch the sneering lips and hear the caustic jibes which baffled and belaboured his Soviet colleague, an intellectual no-holds barred, which brought Gladwyn Jebb to the top place in the American T.V. popularity polls, a position, I have always been told, which he shared with a Turkish all-in wrestler. No public servant of any country ever achieved a higher point of fame than that! I do not mock his achievement or underrate its importance. The world at that time was afraid of the Soviet Union, uncertain of its intentions and sometimes too careful not to offer it any provocation. Gladwyn's consummate self-assurance at the Security Council gave the world courage. It was possible, after all, to stand up to the Russian, not only to stand up to him, but to snub him and browbeat him and make him look a fool. In single combat in that arena Gladwyn was a brilliant victor.

The home civil servant, by the nature of his job, is out of the limelight. His endless industry, his intellectual energy, his tireless exercise of objective thinking, his unremitting service to his political masters, are unseen and unheard. As I have shown, most of them like it that way. I wonder what Norman Brook, if he could have watched it from a cloud, would have thought of his own memorial service—the Abbey thronged with the most prominent men from every walk of life, the Queen represented, the lesson read by a former Prime Minister, all the solemn majesty of prayer and music and in every heart tributes of honour and of respect. He would have been surprised and inwardly tormented with emotion and gratitude, all of it concealed, perhaps, under some critical comment about the phraseology of one of the prayers.

Chapter III

THE FIGHTING MAN

When the battle is joined then the power, the ultimate power of life and death, lies with the commanders. 'No parleying now, but out instantly all you can', says Cromwell, the General, and with rash folly Lord Raglan sends a whole brigade to their death. Upon the orders of Wolfe the Heights of Abraham are stormed and he shares the death to which his orders have exposed others. The Commander-in-Chief, Bomber Command, by the exercise of his direct authority, sends bomber crews to certain death in the fire of the German cities which they have lit up. Nelson ignores a signal and men are pulverized and drowned. Haig, sitting erect and inaccessible in a French château, signs an order which will cause sixty thousand British casualties, twenty thousand of them killed, on a single day. The examples can be multiplied and any Englishman who has commanded any forces in war, on sea, land or air, can be said to have exercised this terrible power, more direct and more decisive than the power of any civilian.

But is that so? Where is the ultimate responsibility? The Nuremberg trial showed how hard it is to pinpoint this. Everyone is acting under the orders of someone else or initiating action in accordance with the sovereign will of the people. There is always a let-out; but in the mind of the soldier there is no doubt at all who gave the order which has suddenly exposed him to mortal danger. He knows where to put the blame, and as he is probably a citizen soldier he will carry back with him into civvy street, if he survives, a superficial notion that Generals and Admirals and Air Marshals like war and enjoy the power which it puts into their bloody grasp. In a militaristic state this might conceivably be true, but in Germany, which to men of my age had seemed just that, history will show that the German Army were opposed to the menacing ambitions of Hitler but had not the unity nor the courage to prevent them. In this country it has never been true. The armed forces in peace time are usually neglected and sometimes derided. They are regarded as unproductive, especially by those who spend the energies of a lifetime in finding profitable methods of selling what nobody wants or needs. The Navy, it is true, has always had a warm corner in the public heart, the Royal Air Force is still regarded as a newcomer, and the Army is instinctively felt to be the traditional descendant of Cromwell's standing army, mistrusted and unpopular. In fact today the fighting Services are designed to keep the peace; that is their role, honourable and respected and understood by the intelligent and sensitive men who control them. Anybody who seriously supposes that it is the top brass which stimulates war and takes delight in carnage would do well to study history with closer attention. Lord Kinross, in his life of Ataturk, wisely says with regard to the Chanak affair, 'one of the occasions (not unusual in history) where the generals were the peacemakers and the politicians the warmongers.' That is well said and would be clearly understood if one was able to meet some of the generals, listen to their discussions, and take a look at them in their private homes.

In these latter days Field Marshal Montgomery has become a legend and his *obiter dicta* are regarded as either oracular or absurd beyond belief. His attitude of utter self-assurance and his unlimited confidence in the correctness of his opinions provoke in younger men amazement rather than admiration. They cannot believe that it is really true that, when some young man happens to say that he was born in 1942 the Field-Marshal will immediately comment in his terse and cocky fashion, 'Oh! I was killing Germans by then'. But it is true, and he says it as if he were recalling some glorious days of slaughter on the moors of Yorkshire or Scotland. It is not true, however, that Monty is bloodthirsty and if he attempts to give that impression it is one of his boyish affectations. He knows, as any commander ought to know, that his soldiers must be trained and tempered to take life and to give it; but of all the great Commanders Monty was perhaps the most cautious, the most reluctant to take a risk which might result in a fruitless sacrifice of men's lives. He obstinately refused to engage Rommel until he was fully satisfied that his soldiers were better equipped than the enemy. He was groping and slow, or so his critics allege, in his follow-up after the Alamein victory. If he was, it was again his solicitude for his soldiers, his determination not to expose them to the dangers of weak lines of communication. This attitude is characteristic of all the commanders I ever knew or read of, but at the same time they combined with their compassion the flinty resolve that danger must be faced and overcome and that, if the directive given to them necessitated the sacrifice of human beings, the sacrifice must be made and the directive carried out. Responsibilities in war do not sit lightly upon the shoulders of military men, of many of whom it can be said that 'their master-bias leans to home-felt pleasures and to gentle scenes'. Yet I have often wondered if this can in truth be said of Monty, in spite of illustrations in his Memoirs of the author 'enjoying the evening life at Isington Mill'. He has never been willing to surrender the power—power, is it, or limelight?—which he enjoyed for so long, and 'the evening of life at Isington Mill' seems to me a false picture of this remarkable man, while Lord Alanbrooke, the toughest and most determined of all CIGS, allowed nothing in the evening of his life to deflect his attention from the bird population of his home at Hartley Wintney, not twenty miles away.

There was a fundamental difference between these two men. The outbreak of the Second World War brought them to positions of great prominence. Like all dedicated soldiers Brooke hoped that his brief command of a Corps before Dunkirk would lead in the end to higher positions of direct command as our fortunes improved. That is the natural ambition of almost all professional soldiers, to attain a position of supreme command, from which to exercise power over multitudes of men and, in a limited sense, over the course of events. There is also the lurking anxiety to avoid the smear of cowardice which has disfigured the reputation of Staff Officers from Shakespeare's popinjay who so much offended Hotspur, through the same suave types, who contributed to the *Disenchantment* of C. E. Montague, to the chair-borne Whitehall warriors, with whom I shared the unspoken suspicions of Desert Rats and D-Day heroes. But Brooke was obliged, by force of circumstances and the orders of a higher power, to remain as CIGS from 1 December, 1941, till well after the end of the war. After all the CIGS was not only the highest Staff Officer in the whole Empire but also the acknowledged Head of the

Army. That would be good enough for most people and it was, of course, 'good enough' for Brooke in the sense that it brought him immense responsibilities, and the most direct influence with the Prime Minister and probably a greater share of power in the conduct of the war than any other single official, civilian or military, in any of the Allied countries. Readers of his diaries know all this. They know the fevered arguments, the tortured disputation, the nervous exercise of patience and self-control, breaking out from time to time into hot and scarcely controlled anger. The soldier's training is designed to enable him to give advice to his superiors, to understand advice given him from below, to reach his conclusion, to make a decision and to see it carried out at once. In the world of Whitehall even in war-time, things cannot proceed just like that. The politicians have strongly-held views on strategy; they have an eye on the post-war world; they have to listen to their allies, consult them, give way to them here and there. In a world war there is no simple, single-minded policy.

If 1940 was our finest hour, it was also in some ways our easiest, with no ally to consult or to object, just a violent enemy to repel. A few days after Brooke took office the surprise attack upon Pearl Harbor took place and that criminal catastrophe, while it gave us the hope of ultimate victory, complicated beyond understanding the processes of planning, decision and execution—a complication which had started with the embracing of our Russian ally (but not friend) in June, 1941. Brooke, when he entered the War Office on 1 December, 1941, must have thought the prospect militarily very bleak indeed. When, in a few days, the entry of the United States into the war changed that bleakness into a faint dawn of hope, he may have felt some quickening of his spirit, but at that moment he could have had no idea of the battering and bewildering complexities of the life ahead of him—the sulky obstinacy of de Gaulle, the thankless grimaces of the Russians and their insatiable demands, the green inexperience of a few of his American colleagues, the pert and insubordinate behaviour of some British generals, the daily triangular difficulty of producing a strategic policy which would satisfy Portal and first Pound and then Cunningham and which would finally convince the Prime Minister that many of his strategic hunches were not much better than backing zero on the roulette table. It is surprising in many ways that this outstanding man found time each night to commit, in his own hand, his tortured thoughts and feelings to paper. Much less surprising was his desire to get away from it all and with a precise directive in his pocket to command and direct armies to the clear objective of destroying the enemy.

That was never to be. Brooke cherished the wish that, when at long last we were ready to invade France, he would be given the command over all the forces employed. He had the soldier's experience and the soldier's confidence for this formidable task and, as a reward for all his laborious contests against self-assertive politicians and undiscerning allies, he deserved it. The reward could not be given. The United States were contributing far more forces to the invasion of Europe than we were and in these circumstances the politicians had no doubt that the Supreme Commander must be an American. General Brooke, Winston Churchill records, 'bore the great disappointment with soldierly dignity'. Brooke supposed, as everyone did at the time, that the task was to be given to General George Marshall, the Chief of Staff of the United States Army, a man of fine quality, sensitive, imaginative and determined. Though he and Brooke were never nearly so close to each other as Marshall and Dill, Brooke must have felt confidence in the upright strength of Marshall's character, his complete integrity and his intellectual power. He may have questioned, with some reason, the extent of Marshall's military experience in the field and his ability to handle the multitude of major tactical and strategic questions which crowd in upon a Supreme Commander in wide-spread operations and demand immediate decision. His chagrin cannot have been mitigated when the appointment went to General Eisenhower, an officer of far less natural ability and far rougher quality than Marshall, but now at any rate with the varied experience of operations in North Africa and the Mediterranean firmly in his knapsack. After all I wonder if Brooke would have handled his American Army Commanders with the patience and tact which Eisenhower displayed towards the British.

It is clear enough from his revealing diaries, those fiery particles thrown off from an overstrained and over-heated

76

centre, that Brooke did not altogether enjoy the power which the position of CIGS gave him. 'I have just about reached the end of my tether . . .' 'I am quite exhausted . . .' There are frequent notes of despair, and throughout is a thread of real distaste for the intrigues and goings-on of politicians. There is an occasional expression of satisfaction when at long last strategic sense has been made to prevail, and a note of fervent gratitude at the success of Allied arms. But it is the occasional day off which is treasured and loved by this aggressive and irascible soldier:—

'14 May 1944. Spent Sunday at home photographing a marsh tit. These two hours in a hide close to a marsh tit at its nest made Winston and the war disappear in a cloud of smoke. It was like rubbing Aladdin's lamp. I was transplanted to a fairyland and returned infinitely refreshed and recreated.'

There is the Happy Warrior, and if Brooke could have exchanged the airless streets of London, its shabby unpainted buildings, its devastated bomb sites, and all the quarrelling and disputing, the frustrations and delays of 'war at the top', for a tactical H.Q. in France he might have had rather more frequent visitations of these moments of bliss even in the midst of the noise and smoke of battle over which he would then have had supreme control.

Monty was a horse of quite a different colour. Though he shared with Brooke the professional skill and the professional pride of a dedicated soldier, the ambitions and the springs of action seem to me quite distinct. Monty loved a full blaze of publicity; Brooke would have endured it, somewhat coolly, if it had been a part of his duty. Monty without any doubt used his flair for self-advertisement to very good ends. On his arrival in the Western Desert he saw at once that the Eighth Army, though a tried instrument of war, had lost confidence in itself and in its commanders. Within a very short time Monty had restored that confidence. His arrival had an electrifying effect, high-ranking New Zealand officers have told me. 'We were bewildered and uncertain,' they said, 'until he came but thereafter we could have beaten any enemy.' He achieved this revolution in morale, first by making sure as I have said, that the equipment of the Eighth Army was superior to that of the

77

Afrika Corps, and next by a display of personal eccentricities and vulgar egoism, which Brooke would have disdained, but which took the trick, and it was a trick which had to be taken.

The arts of the showman were perhaps less needed when it came to the invasion of France in 1944. By then the Army was self-confident and resilient—thanks to Monty—but of course in operations of the first magnitude all armies need leadership, not only tactical and strategic leadership, but human leadership, the leadership that makes every soldier feel that up at the top is a remote and powerful figure, very brave and very clever, who knows all the answers and is certain to bring off a victory. Apart from Monty, both Wavell and Alexander had something of this power, and Eisenhower, if he lacked the military experience and the hard remorseless intellect of the great commander, was, nevertheless, skilful at winning loyalty and devotion from his subordinates. Whether Brooke or Marshall had this power it is impossible to say because they were never put to the test. Perhaps after all destiny had put the right pieces in the right places. Monty certainly could not have filled Brooke's role, and whatever their friendship may have been in the 'evening of life' Winston and Monty could not have worked closely together as Prime Minister and CIGS for more than a week. Indeed Monty himself says in his Memoirs about his two years (1946-48) as CIGS, 'When I recall those days I often think that Whitehall was my least happy theatre of war. It did not provide "my sort of battle" . . . I was pretty unpopular when I left Whitehall to become an international soldier'. That is unfortunately quite true and no two men were gladder to see him go than his two colleagues on the Chiefs of Staff Committee, Lord Tedder, the Chief of the Air Staff, and Sir John Cunningham, the First Sea Lord. For many months I was a witness to their deliberations, in the same capacity in which I had attended meetings of the war-time Chiefs of Staff— namely to act as a link between them and the Joint Planning Staff, of which I was the Secretary. The contrast was alarming. I have described elsewhere the intense pressure of work which afflicted Brooke, Portal and Cunningham in war, their daily deliberations, the intellectual struggle with difficulties, the disputes, the dreadful urgency to reach decisions; but underlying all that was a determination to achieve a unity of view.

They were strong men with strong opinions but always ready to listen to each other and to listen to advice from their own staffs and their inter-Service staffs. When Monty succeeded Brooke as CIGS in 1946, the achievement of unified aims and harmonious co-operation became impossible; and the main reason for this was that Monty was not in the habit of listening to anybody except his own closest personal advisers. He was not interested in what Tedder thought and hardly disguised his contempt for the somewhat melancholy interventions of Cunningham. As for the Joint Planning Staff, they were just a pack of fools, whose reports should be completely ignored— a prejudiced opinion which did not, however, prevent him from occasionally announcing their conclusions as if they were his own. That was just the trouble. It was he who must develop the arguments, he must reach the conclusions and make the decisions. He must have all the credit for himself and the power and the glory were not to be shared with anybody else. He could not work in any other way. He knew instinctively that it was no good telling soldiers that he was transmitting to them decisions which had been reached in a committee, that the decisions had been agreed by other equal Powers; that was no good, that would lead to a loss of confidence. The soldiers had faith in him, because they thought he made the decisions and, if they had thought otherwise, their confidence would have waned and disappeared. In the conditions of war his attitude was unquestionably right, but in Whitehall in peace-time it was disastrous. I can see that ill-starred Chiefs of Staff Committee now, sitting in what had been the Prime Minister's map room just inside the Storey's Gate entrance to the then Ministry of Defence, Tedder in the Chair, Cunningham on his right and Monty on his left, all three of them caught in a sort of spell of hatred and spite which they could not break. It was Monty's doing, of course. He hated the whole machine. He detested committees and, as it happened, he detested Tedder, a feeling fully reciprocated. He did not want the machine to work. He believed in the principle of the Supreme Commander, the Chief of Defence Staff, and it was towards the establishment of that system that he used every weapon of malice and intrigue in his capacious quiver. He failed to bring it off. The three war-time Chiefs of Staff, with Pug Ismay in attendance, had worked supremely well. Why change it? Now it has been changed, as the world well knows, but I have heard no evidence to suggest that it has worked any better.

Anyway Monty went off, as he says, to be 'an international soldier' and for ten more years he did excellent service as Deputy Supreme Commander in NATO, a job which he would not have relished or done well in war-time. As it was he used his unrivalled experience and prestige in the right cause. He understood clearly the strategic needs and the international difficulties of NATO and he was given freedom, outside the normal chain of command, to preach the gospel in all the countries of this alliance. He had the cause very much at heart, and the position, though in a sense subservient to a succession of American Supreme Commanders, gave him enough independent prestige and importance to satisfy that insatiable desire within him for power, personal power upon which the limelight played.

A less famous personality was Wavell, but in the minds and memories of many men the outstanding Commander of the war. It would be difficult to defend this estimate by statistics— a series of initial victories against all the odds, followed by one disaster after another and finally a terrible loss of confidence in the heart of the Prime Minister, who had never had much anyway, and great fatigue and self-mistrust in the heart of Wavell himself. Winston's lack of confidence, amounting almost to mistrust and dislike, was a good deal fortified by an incident which throws important light on the character of Wavell—his humanity, his solicitude for those under his command, his merciful use of power, and his fearless attitude to rash anger in those above him. When British Somaliland was evacuated in August, 1940, this necessary but regrettable operation was carried out, under Wavell's orders, by General Godwin-Austen with very few British casualties and at considerable loss to the Italians. Winston was outraged by the small number of British casualties thinking it was conclusive evidence of inefficiency and cowardice, and sent a cable to Wavell ordering him to suspend Godwin-Austen and saying that a court of inquiry should be held. Wavell replied refusing to suspend Godwin-Austen, deploring a court of inquiry as disastrous to morale and concluding with the striking dictum that 'a big butcher's bill was not necessarily evidence of good tactics'. Winston was incensed by this remark, but no more was heard about suspensions and courts of inquiry. 'Quite small light table beer . . . a good journeyman soldier who knows his job reasonably well, not afraid of responsibility but not seeking it . . .', that is how Wavell described himself to me. In some respects that is an over-modest estimate, but in others somewhere near the truth. He was not afraid of responsibility; he carried it manfully and often successfully in the Middle East for nearly three years. While he carried it he proved himself a good deal stronger than 'quite small light table beer'. He was the first, perhaps the only, British General whom the Germans feared and respected. In February 1939 he delivered the Lee Knowles Lectures at Trinity College Cambridge, unnoticed at the time but published later and translated into several languages including German. Rommel's extensive understanding of 'Generals and Generalship' was in some part derived from these Lectures, a copy of which, carefully annotated, he carried about with him in the Western Desert. There is bitter irony in the reflection that not only did Rommel learn something from Wavell but the German High Command learnt a great deal from Charles de Gaulle's *Vers l'armée de métier* published in 1934—a book almost totally ignored by the French.

Wavell, then, was rather better than 'a good journeyman soldier'. He had studied his profession deeply, thought about it and could pronounce upon it in a style of lucid simplicity. He had even considered in 1938 the idea of being an academic soldier, and of applying for the Chichele Professorship of Military History at Oxford University. He abandoned the idea because he could see war not far off; and Oxford lost a potential military historian of great renown, while the nation gained an experienced and confident commander whose professional skill, equable temperament and intellectual grasp guided our destinies through the first troubled and uncertain years. Wavell, like all men, needed some sort of relaxation from those crushing responsibilities of which 'he was not afraid but did not seek'. Brooke found it in a rapt contemplation of the marsh tit, Monty found it—no, he did not find it, he did not seem to need it—and Wavell found it in literature, both reading

81

it and making it. He was adept at the few lines of light verse, which relieve a period of tension and bring sensitive people back to the conviction that, even in war, 'life should not be taken seriously all the time', as Lord David Cecil once put it; he finished his excellent biography of Allenby during the war, and also during the war published his anthology *Other Men's Flowers,* his large and varied collection of the poetry he knew by heart and loved. I am sure Wavell loved power less than Brooke and much less than Monty, and perhaps that is why his success as a Commander was short-lived and rather brittle. The high ability and the deep devotion to duty were abundant, the professional skill was of the highest quality, but did he enjoy the exercise of the great power which lay in his grasp? Monty enjoyed every minute of it and that is why, in spite of my deep sympathies and predilections in other directions, I believe Monty was the best British Commander in the war. Moreover Monty was loquacious, eager to talk and expound and admonish with fluent and staccato confidence, his discourse unlimited except by the paucity of his vocabulary and the narrow confines of his imagination. Wavell, on the other hand, was taciturn to the point of rudeness. Some members of Attlee's Cabinet, quite wrongly, thought him so high-hat that he could not be bothered to explain to the Cabinet his vice-regal estimate of the political situation in India—so unlike Monty who when instructed by the same Cabinet to carry out some operation or other would respond in cocksure fashion, 'Yes, of course it can be done. Quite simple so long as there is no belly-aching from you'. Many men and women withdrew from Wavell's presence without a sign or a nod that he had paid the slightest attention to them. If you sat next to him at dinner it was very hard going, one gambit after another defeated, either by a refusal to move for an hour or by a sudden brilliant move which silenced you in a long-sustained search for a worthy reply. 'Journeyman soldier', that is an inadequate description and John Connell was right to add to the title of the first volume of the biography of this great man 'Scholar and Soldier'—the two intentions and ambitions intertwined, the love of history and learning which apart from throwing a light from the past upon the actors on his stage enriched and deepened his whole personality, and the unremitting acquisition of professional skills and the selfless devotion to the soldiers under his command, which are characteristic of the best type of officer. John Connell had got the values right and he aptly and generously estimated the depths and the sincerities of this noble man.

I can say nothing at first hand of Earl Alexander of Tunis as a Commander. My only contact with him was during his period as Minister of Defence, and here he was without doubt wrongly cast. It is a fact, however, that he was Winston's choice. When Winston returned to power in October, 1951, he himself assumed the position of Minister of Defence, a position from which he had driven and directed the Chiefs of Staff and the Commanders-in-Chief during the war, a position, moreover, which he loved above any other. He was most reluctant to surrender it and apply himself more closely to the economic and industrial affairs of the country, but he was persuaded to consent on the condition, formed in his own mind that he could withdraw Alexander from Canada, where he was Governor-General, and give him the job. This took time but when at last it was accomplished it meant at least that the Prime Minister had complete confidence in his Minister of Defence. In times of stress, when decisions to use British arms or exhibit British strength had to be taken, Winston was accustomed to say in almost awestruck tones, 'Field Marshal, we shelter behind your splendid name'. It cannot have been less surprising to Alexander than it was to me, that this assertive and over-confident man should defer to him and seek his opinion, which was orthodox and correct within the terms of his brief, but could become rather naive when stretched beyond it. In this attitude of respect from a greater to a lesser man there must have been many factors—the comparative careers at Harrow (though not of course at the same time), the one that of a fine, well-born aristocratic type of boy, good at everything including cricket, at which in those days excellence was judged equivalent to virtue and leadership of the highest quality; the other rather discontented, rebellious and out of it, but slightly envious of those glorious men, agile, confident and clever, who ruled without question the ambitions and hopes of the lesser fry. And then the respective careers—Winston a brief period in the 4th Hussars, enough to give him a taste for the trappings, the sporting activities and the rather smart and splendid appurtenances of the military life as it was then lived, followed by stirring adventures in military journalism rather shocking to the severe orthodoxy of the regimental soldier, and after that politics, the knockabout excitement, the chances and mischances, the ups and downs, power at one moment and impotence the next, the constant argument and controversy, exaggerated rhetoric to make a party point, no steady course to win a sure reward; Alexander on the other hand making steadfast unassuming progress, admired and trusted by every member of his profession, a soldier's soldier, gaining without fuss or scramble the highest positions in the Army and holding them, as to the manner born, good-looking and of fine bearing, with a natural unobtrusive charm that won the complete fidelity and loyalty of all the troops, of whatever nation, which at any time came under his command. I can see why Alexander exercised a sort of magnetism over Winston. He was so many things that Winston never could have been, though his great abilities were by comparison modest; but that could be said of most men. I should think that Alexander was not in the least concerned about acquiring power, but power came to him as if it were his by right and he seemed to use it effortlessly. He commanded Allied Armies drawn from many nations and hardly ever was there a murmur of disapproval or distrust. Winston would have loved to be in those shoes, emulating with all the panoply of personal grandeur the manners and exploits of his most famous ancestor. Military pomp and splendour had a great fascination for him.

When I turn my thoughts about power and about powerful personalities from the Army to the other two Services I am on less familiar ground. At my own level I knew officers from the Navy and the R.A.F. quite as well as I knew officers from the Army. I knew their particular points of view, the very special troubles which afflicted them. I knew their attitudes to these problems—the confident assertiveness of the Navy, bred by its illustrious inheritance and its nation-wide renown; and I knew equally well and liked just as warmly the throw-away, devil-may-care attitude of the R.A.F., bred in them by the brief decisive boldness of the Battle of Britain and the certainty that long and pompous arguments and elaborate reports with precise conclusions and recommendations were no answer to a lethal power that came swiftly, and usually unannounced, from a black horizon or a cloud in the sky above you. I was a planner and they were all planners with me. The plan must be sound and realistic, the Army thought, based on solid logistic calculations, economical of manpower and heavily reinforced by masses of up-to-date equipment. It must be flexible and daring, the Navy thought, based upon British sea power which would permit a multiplicity of sharp attacks here and there rather than a long plodding struggle over mud and mountains. The R.A.F. thought all plans rather absurd; it did not happen like that. Somebody suddenly attacked you and you hit back; or you took a lot of aeroplanes and delivered a lot of bombs on the enemy, and that was just the job and no help was needed from anyone else. I exaggerate, of course, but in general these were the respective first principles from which the arguments began and continued until a satisfactory and realistic synthesis emerged. That was the job of the Joint Planning Staff—the inter-service staff which served the Chiefs of Staff Committee—to examine every factor likely to affect any plan or any recommendation for action and the various interests likely to be affected by the plan, to argue every consideration from every angle, not only the angle of the three fighting Services but also of the Foreign Office, the Ministry of War Transport, the Ministry of Production and so on, to argue critically and at great speed, and then for the representatives of the three fighting Services, the Directors of Plans, to come up with a synthetic and practical solution which the Chiefs of Staff might be likely to accept. I served many Directors of Plans and many outstanding staff officers beneath them and I doubt very much if any one of them at any time felt that the compensation for days and nights of exhausting disputes and frustrating quests for solutions was a sense of power. A historical judgment would allot to the Joint Planning Staff a considerable amount of power and influence over the conduct of the war at the centre. At the time the uppermost sensation amongst the Planners themselves was relief to have got the thing done and submitted in time; nothing can wait in war. There was scarcely a moment to watch the practical effect of the recommendations made before several other strategic and operational problems crowded in and the wheels of that machine, never at rest, revolved violently once again.

I have exaggerated the respective points of view of the Staff

85

Officers of the three different Services, as if they were predictable and always the same. That is quite wrong, and, when I think back to my time as the Secretary of the Joint Planning Staff, in my mind and my memory I distinguish the many Directors of Plans I served, not so much by their Service as by their personalities, their individual quality. There was one of high intellectual ability, ready and able to argue effectively with the Foreign Office representative about international factors of the highest importance, in his leisure time, hardly existent then, adept at the pianoforte, a man of taste and discrimination, sensitive looks and sensitive attitudes. He was, in fact, a sailor, who subsequently rose to the position of First Sea Lord and during his time in that office died suddenly of a thrombosis, not unexpected in a man who not only gave himself without reservation to his own Service but on the side cultivated the arts and sought intellectual interests in matters outside his brief, sparing himself nothing in the mental, physical and spiritual efforts to be a complete man. His closest friend in those days was his R.A.F. colleague, a brave and devoted professional like all these fighting Service officers, but beyond all this sensitive above the common, discriminating, fastidious, rightly assessing the values for which he was quite prepared to die and tough enough to make others less courageous face the same risk. Both these men I grew to like and admire very much, neither of them in the least like the public image of their Service. Both are to me examples of how a man may rise above even the high level of his tried and tested profession and give manhood a supplementary and exciting significance. They liked each other very much and when they were joined by a new Army Director of Plans they were at first a little less than friendly. He was a man with a sharp intellectual edge and a manner which often failed to conceal his scorn for what he thought rubbish and his impatience with long and fruitless argument. Moreover he had a full measure of self-confidence and an evident conviction that when it came to plans and staff work the Army was usually right. The self-confidence was not misplaced and when it was urgent to reach a decisive conclusion he was more often right than wrong. This was soon recognised and admired by the other two and the team became a very strong one, much trusted and respected by the Chiefs of

Staff. The unity of the Joint Planning Staff Trinity was compact and firm, the only dent caused by the slight shudder of the two firmly established and highly cultivated friends at some lack of grace in the formidably efficient newcomer. A part of my job, I used to think, was to bring them to agreement and if possible make them like each other. All three are now dead, but for me they are very much alive with their sharp disagreements, their caustic rejoinders, their continuous questing and probing, their occasional spontaneous laughter at some absurd misunderstanding, and underlying it all their united determination to arrive at a sensible and practical solution which they could submit to the Chiefs of Staff.

Chiefs of Staff and Commanders-in-Chief in peace-time are unknown figures, quite as unknown and unsung as their Civil Service equivalents, but in war they assume great importance and achieve great renown. Their Civil Service equivalents continue in their dimmed and dutiful anonymity. But of course the quality of the men continues to be the same, although it is quite true that in war this quality is tried and tested in circumstances of exceptional hazard and intensity. Men whose names were never heard before become beacons and the reputations of other men, much valued in peace-time, are gradually and strangely extinguished. One such was Ironside, who apart from his name seemed to have all the qualities and courage of a war-time leader—an immense man, more than six feet four inches tall and large and robust in proportion, an experienced fighting soldier, a gifted linguist and so versed in intelligence that he was said to be the original of Richard Hannay in John Buchan's exciting studies in espionage. And yet as CIGS for the first nine months of the war and then as Commander-in-Chief Home Forces until July, 1940, he made no mark at all. He was quickly superseded and passed into a limbo and nobody would have guessed that he lived till 1959. He was forgotten, a spent force, put aside almost twenty years before his death, found in the trials of war not to be up to the test, in spite of the qualities which had brought him to the top in peace-time. It is hard to account for such failures by men educated to exercise power who at the critical moment, when brought up against issues of supreme importance, become halting, confused and uncertain. It was one of Winston's outstanding qualities that he was able to detect in others the decline of their grip and authority and to send them away, before it was too late, to less exacting jobs. The tragedy was that he himself had no sensation, no conception of the decline in his own powers.

It is perhaps true that Sir Dudley Pound continued in the office of First Sea Lord beyond his term of profitable service, but Winston decided to leave his resignation in the hands of death or at least of serious illness. In September, 1943, Pound had a stroke and offered the Prime Minister his resignation; this was accepted and a merciful death came very soon. He had without doubt persevered beyond the limits of his strength, not because he loved position and power, but through a dominating sense of duty, which made him feel that, however tired he was, he must never yield. For myself I hardly ever saw Pound in the flesh and was never anywhere near enough to him to form my own judgment. Alan Brooke in the dreadful days of February, 1942, thought Pound's handling of the Chiefs of Staff Committee, of which he was then Chairman, tragically fumbling and inept. With Pound as Chairman, Brooke commented to his diary 'it is impossible for the Chiefs of Staff Committee to perform the functions it should in the biggest Imperial war we are ever likely to be engaged in. He is asleep during seventy-five per cent of the time he should be working', looking as Brooke observed elsewhere 'like an old parrot asleep on his perch'. Later Brooke felt this estimate harsh and ungenerous and wrote 'Had I known that he was probably already suffering from the disease he died from, I should certainly not have made these remarks . . . they are not intended as any personal criticism of this very fine sailor who at one time was a very sick man and who continued working till he died of overwork. He was the most charming of colleagues to work with had it not been for this failing of slowness and sleepiness'. Within less than a month Brooke had succeeded Pound as Chairman, though Pound struggled on as First Sea Lord till the autumn of 1943. This was a case in which Winston should have acted sooner. It would not have been difficult. Pound stayed because he thought it was his duty and not because he loved his place.

These were great men, conspicuous in their profession, but once they were boys embarking upon a career. What were their feelings then and was it a love of power which decided their choice? They are older than I am and I do not know at all what motive drove them forward. Monty simply tells us, 'My father had always hoped that I would become a clergyman. That did not happen and I well recall his disappointment when I told him that I wanted to be a soldier . . . If I had my life over again I would not choose differently. I would be a soldier.' This explanation discloses nothing more about his motive than a simple wish. Wavell, on the other hand, thought it beyond his strength of character to opt for any other profession, in spite of the objection of the Headmaster that he was wasting his brains. 'I never felt any special inclination to a military career,' writes Wavell, 'but it would have taken more independence of character than I possessed at the time to avoid it. Nearly all my relations were in the Army. I had been brought up amongst soldiers; and my father, while professing to give me complete liberty of choice, was determined that I should be a soldier. I had no particular bent towards any other profession, and I took the line of least resistance'. That is characteristically candid. Often it was this family tradition, sometimes the imperious call of war, denying all other options, sometimes an early choice imposed and unquestioned, sometimes an escape from higher, more arduous and more frequent obstacles to a different career. In their days a sailor was designated and devoted from the age of 12, and the First War swallowed up many men who might have preferred any profession to the profession of arms. But whatever the circumstances, I asked myself, was it a longing for power which directed them into the armed Services? I taxed my memory to think of my own contemporaries and of those whom I taught and advised in the 1920s and 30s. What were their motives and their ambitions?

I grew up in the shadow of the First World War. It had already started when I went as a small boy to Radley and before I had been two years at school the dreadful slaughter on the Somme began. At once the war came nearer to me and to my friends and contemporaries. Boys who had left school a term or two before, it seemed, boys, much more than names to us, living personalities, liked or admired, or feared perhaps, for some special individual qualities, were killed or wounded; and the Roll of Honour, which the Warden read out daily in

Chapel, grew longer, more poignant and more intimate every day. These young men, in the glory of their youth, were not in search of power. They were called to positions of fleeting power over handfuls of weary, cursing, frightened soldiers and in the brief exercise of this power became a reluctant sacrifice for causes which they could not have understood. Those of us who were younger and were still at Radley watched our names come nearer to the top of the list of the proscribed and tried to steel ourselves to do our duty when our turn came round. But we were very young and the love of life and movement and beauty, the affection and admiration which we felt for each other, the splendour of our boyhood could not be altogether put aside and obliterated by the grim realities of these most terrible years. For most of the time we chattered and laughed about nothing, enjoying the warm company of our friends, sharing secret aspirations and fears, our minds and our feelings set upon the present, that very day in our existence, without a passing thought for war and death. Now and then on Sunday evenings, spent in our Housemaster's drawing room, we would talk with him about the war and about the peace that would follow the war, the chance that would come to put right social injustice and inequality and build a nobler nation in a securer world. And then we would walk back through the dark night to our dormitories—two or three of us, with arms linked in an intimacy of thought and feeling, wondering and groping for the truth and the meaning. There was no choice for us. When the clock struck we would have to go and perhaps add our lives to the sacrificial list, following the example of boys we had loved.

There was a boy, about two years my senior, whom I knew as intimately as one human being can know another. He grew up without a thought of the army in his head. His ambitions lay elsewhere. His father died young; and he was brought up in real penury, trained to habits of strict and austere economy, but never permitted to forget that a life of natural dignity and high standards of conduct can be achieved without the aid of money. If the background of his boyhood was simple and severe, it was also cultured and continuously softened by love and laughter. His mother was artistic and musical, herself brought up by a scholarly father to a love and admiration for

90

literature and learning. She had the artist's eye, percipient and sensitive, and she taught her son to watch and observe, to love butterflies and flowers, to read deeply, to explore the country-side, to probe the history of old churches, to be sensitive to all his surroundings and to live his life to the full. He reacted with joy. He loved her and shared her tastes and her delights. He was gay and clever and goodlooking, a king of nonsense and of laughter. Somehow he must go to Oxford. He would get scholarships; and after that, well! Perhaps the Diplomatic Service and the gradual restoration of the family fortunes. But in December, 1917, he was 18 years old and there was no longer any option of careers. The army claimed him and disciplined him for the brief horror of that soulless war. He learnt to command others, to exercise power over human beings, to lead them by gentle influence and brave example. In the stark obliteration of beauty, in the shuddering fear of trench warfare, divorced from the warmth and love of his home and of his family, he achieved his manhood—and lost it, suddenly and violently, as a German bullet shattered his face just ten days before Western Europe found an uneasy peace.

Of the boys I taught between the wars, not very many chose the Services as a profession. It was the fashion to seek careers in civil life and at least until the rise of Hitler it was expected that there would be no further violent rupture of the peace and that men would pursue their professions and their occupa-tions in security from external dangers. I daresay I encouraged, in my own circle, this drift away from the profession of arms and certainly it was not till 1933 that I myself felt it right and necessary to apply for a commission in the Territorial Army. In the event nearly all the boys whose friendship I enjoyed at St Edward's School between 1924 and 1935 found themselves up to the hilt in the Second World War and their record, especially in the R.A.F., was quite outstanding. They had a striking example to follow. When I joined the staff of St Edward's School in 1924, amongst some interesting and able boys there was one who immediately commanded attention and has continued to command it ever since—Douglas Bader, an individual cast in a heroic mould. When he joined the R.A.F. in 1928 he was seeking not power, but adventure, and he soon found it. In the pursuit of adventure he acquired power of an unusual kind. By his dauntless triumph over crippling misfortune and blank despair he has inspired others to face their disasters with the same spirit. Moreover he is the most lively example I know that the child is in fact father of the man. It is more than 40 years since he left school and during that time he has not only cheated death and scoffed at danger, he has been subjected to the incessant gaze of an admiring public, he has been welcomed and flattered in every country and in every society, he is acquainted with Kings and Bishops, anxious to pay him their respect, and he has treated them, just as he treats everyone else, with an unbridled friendliness over-riding pomp and protocol, about which he knows nothing and cares less. I saw him not long since at some summer function at his old school. He sat in the centre of a group and as I watched him the years fell away. I was a young schoolmaster and he was in his vigorous unscarred adolescence. His face was aglow, his eyes bright with gaiety and impishness. He talked, just as he had always talked, with exuberant humour, the anecdote and the rejoinders designed to shock but never to wound. The level of the conversation—if it could be called conversation—was never slow or dull but delicate and tricky, brittle at times, just as it had always been. How far can I go? Will this young schoolmaster assume the authority of his black gown and silly hat and pipe me down? Will the ladies in this group turn aside in shocked dismay? These are issues which he judges finely; but he gets away with it as he has always done and always will do.

In all my examples of the fighting man from Brooke to Bader there is not one who used the military career as a stepping stone to political power. It is true that Alexander became Minister of Defence in Churchill's second Government, but he did so with great reluctance, I suspect, and with the utmost diffidence. It was not the sort of power he was looking for and he had little idea what use to make of it. Wavell became Viceroy of India, a position he wanted because of his love of India and his interest in its problems. He had been C-in-C India and had commanded Indian divisions in the Middle East. Perhaps he felt this experience qualified him for a supremely difficult job and in any case his appointment to this great office was public recognition that in spite of all the disputes, defeats and disappointments in the Middle East and the Far East he had not lost the confidence of the Prime Minister. His Vice-regal days were numbered and perhaps it was no sorrow to Wavell when the final processes of disengagement were handed to another. It is rare in the history of this country for military men to be attracted by political ambitions. Wellington had some experience of political life before his dedication to the soldier's life in India and subsequently in the Peninsula; and the confidence which his run of victories inspired made it inevitable that he should be expected to show the same infallibility, the same poise and self-assurance in civilian affairs. His political career was by no means an unmitigated success. The experiment of putting Kitchener into the Cabinet as a sort of overriding War Lord in 1914 was almost a disaster. All the great military leaders in the last war were determined to keep out of politics once it was over. While Eisenhower became President of the United States, Montgomery remained a professional soldier and Brooke continued to observe the marsh tits at Hartley Wintney.

In France it is different. General Bonaparte became Emperor of France and uplifted and stimulated the nation through a dozen years of military conquest and glory. The army in France, throughout the nineteenth century and after, occupied a far more important and influential position in the national life than ever the British army did in this country. It is not therefore quite so surprising that an almost unknown French Brigadier should have arisen like a Phoenix from the ashes of 1940. The courage, the consummate assurance, the cheek of the man in those days filled many of us with an admiration amounting to awe. I remember going to a small cocktail party in the Ritz in the early days of 1941, given, I think, by the Director of Military Operations in honour of Brigadier de Gaulle. In he stalked, rather late and rather royal, his great height dominating the room, and in spite of his ungainliness, his hock-bottle shoulders, his receding chin and long nose, there was an air of aloof dignity about him. His manner was far from warm and convivial. How could it be different, in such modest company? He was playing his part. In spite of his uniform and badges of rank, he was not just an ordinary French Brigadier to be treated as an equal by British offices of the same rank. His air of condescension showed that he felt he had been uncommonly decent to come along at all. In those days his public appearances were often greeted by polite handclapping from the admiring but normally phlegmatic British. Such unusual manifestations brought no affectionate response from him, but served only to increase his intellectual pride and his obstinate arrogance. De Gaulle became a soldier because he felt that it was through the Army that France would attain the almost mystical greatness and high destiny, which was his lifelong ideal. When in 1940 the Army failed through the incompetence of Generals and politicians, what could he do but take that high destiny into his own hands and unite, as Bonaparte had done, the civil and military powers in his own person? The rest is history. In the context of this chapter it is perhaps of some interest to recall that, although he poured contempt upon the Army—the Army had been wrong on every important issue: 'It was against Dreyfus; it was for Vichy; it was for Algerian integration'—in the days of his apotheosis he still preferred the style Mon Général to M. le Président.

Chapter IV

THE SCHOOLMASTER

Schoolboys and undergraduates spend a lot of their time in a make-believe world. They cannot in their inexperienced freshness know very much about the realities of life, its disappointments, its harsh severities, its limitations and its complexities; and what they do not know they invent in accordance with their fancy. They dream their dreams and see their visions and feel that it is within the power of their generation—as it has never been before—to set things right and to make a new earth and a new heaven. With the same wide-eyed surprise they look upon the men who teach and admonish them. The light of common day has not yet encompassed the human race in drab shades of grey and black and the most ordinary and commonplace of men take strange and lively colours from the eyes of those they teach. In all schools nearly every master is endowed with some outstanding attribute. One killed a man in a game of association football, another is a secret drunkard, another would have been a headmaster long ago if his wife had not been a nymphomaniac; and all have such strange mannerisms, such tricks of voice, such curious attitudes that the whole world must stand amazed at these oddities of creation. Much time is spent in recounting improbable stories about the exploits of these grotesques, and much ingenuity wasted upon imitations of their oracular sayings and their outlandish demeanour. In one famous school the boys spent hours noting down the unusual sayings and the abnormal pronunciations of a certain learned master and then, with far more ingenuity and concentration than they spent on their Latin and Greek compositions or their Ancient History note-books, they compiled—and secretly published—a dictionary of this new and curious language. The school was Winchester and the language Mushri—the language of Moorshead. In another school, close to my heart, a man of considerable learning and discriminating taste was transformed by a very few generations of humorous, light-hearted and flippant pupils into

95

the strangest figure, the victim of rapidly passing moods, impetuous rage accompanied by a futile stamping and an ineffectual surging up and down the room with uncontrolled gown sweeping pens and inkpots in every direction; to be followed almost at once by a fatuous sparkle in the eye, a meaningless brushing of the cheek and some inarticulate silliness—or so we chose to think. But once in a discussion of Christian theories about the value of all forms of life he suddenly enquired, 'Are we then to assume that a sponge is entitled to everlasting life?' Nobody could answer that one and he was left in unusual, and rather embarrassed, command of the field.

I do not suppose that either of these men, on entering the profession of schoolmaster, expected that in a very few years he would be regarded as eccentric and even grotesque and in fact it is unlikely that either of them fully realised what had happened. They were disappointed and frustrated by the inattention and silliness of the boys they taught. They had hoped perhaps to preside effectively over groups of intelligent disciples. They loved the learning which they had acquired and they wanted to pass it on. That can be construed as a desire for power of a sort and there is no doubt at all that the many nineteenth-century headmasters of public schools who were themselves eminent scholars exercised immense power over the minds and lives of their pupils simply through the medium of teaching. This was true of Thomas Arnold, though his chief aim was to inspire in boys moral excellence and his teaching of academic subjects was a means to that end. It was true of Butler and Kennedy, successive headmasters of Shrewsbury, who established the reputation of that school on a strong foundation of fine classical scholarship. Boys went to Shrewsbury because their parents hoped that they would fall under the intellectual influence of its headmaster. At King Edward's School, Birmingham, James Prince Lee, who became headmaster in 1858, was not only a successful teacher in terms of university distinctions gained, but an inspired one whose influence upon his VIth Form was profound. Brooke Foss Westcott, later Bishop of Durham, said of him, 'We might be able to follow him or not; but we were stirred in our work, we felt a little more the claims of duty, the pricelessness of opportunity, the meaning of life. And when I reflect now on all that he did and suggested in the light of my own experience as a teacher, I seem to be able to discern something of my master's secret, the secret in due measure of every teacher's influence. He claimed us from the first as his fellow workers. He made us feel that in all learning we must be active and not receptive only.' Arnold and Lee and, in the same tradition, E. W. Benson at Wellington and Charles Wordsworth at Glenalmond exerted influence and power over the minds and characters of their better or superior pupils, and without any doubt they knew that they exerted this power and they wanted to do so. One of the objects of education was to produce an élite class, so that, equipped with an impenetrable armour of moral and intellectual virtues, it might guide and direct a nation, otherwise made up of thousands of under-privileged persons who had been denied any access to the groves of godliness and good learning. This is a doctrine now despised and rejected. The paternalistic view of society is smudged and smeared; but it is not my purpose in this book to examine the rights and wrongs of this concept of society. My quest is to find the true motive of those men who decide to become schoolmasters and the different ways in which they exert the power and influence which without any doubt this office gives them.

Those nineteenth-century public school headmasters to whom I have already made reference were convinced that their learning, their sense of duty, and their moral and spiritual qualities marked them out as fit to control and inspire the younger generation into whose hands the power of government would fall. They were all young men themselves, still sustained by a proselytising fervour. Arnold was 33 when he was made headmaster of Rugby, Prince Lee 34 when he went to King Edward's School Birmingham, Benson 30 when he was made the first Master of Wellington and Charles Wordsworth 40 when he went to Glenalmond. Butler was only 24 when he went to Shrewsbury, and Kennedy, who followed him, 32. They all of them wanted to exert power and influence over the rising generation, convinced in themselves that their intimate acquaintance with the history, philosophy and literature of Greece and Rome and their proximity in age and outlook to adolescents endowed them with very special qualifications for their great calling. They did in fact exercise a very great influence, irrelevant and misconceived, some modern critics would say, misconceived because of the almost total neglect of scientific subjects, irrelevant because aristocratic rule was already doomed. But the boys who sat under them and surrendered to their influence thought otherwise. There was a very strong bond between these headmasters and their leading pupils, not only intellectual but highly emotional. Sewell at Radley conducted a strange love affair with his boys, especially the sons of the landed gentry, and preached in the chapel highly charged and highly coloured effusions which made the boys of 1860 cry but which would make the boys of today blush with shame. 'Again and again,' he says in a by-no-means uncharacteristic sermon 'when you little ones have come to me, and I have put my hand to your hearts, I have found them beating so violently, and seen tears, before I spoke a word, starting into your eyes, that before I could tell you what I wanted, I have been obliged to put my arms around you, and tell you not to be frightened.' If that is an example of the emotionalism of the time, the following emphasises with striking absurdity the notion of an élite, an aristocratic body by nature ordained to guide and rule. In the course of a sermon Sewell announced that he had told the Senior Prefect to entertain all boys with noble blood in their veins to a special dinner, and went on as follows, 'Be assured, my boys, that this little act and sign, petty as it is, asserts and establishes among us a grand principle of our own welfare here as a great place of education, and for our future conduct in the world . . . Look on the boys who will dine together today—many of them very young—many of them with no personal claim to any particular respect, not with jealousy and contempt, but with manly, honourable, elevating respect for rank. And that feeling carried out into the world will save you alike from the vulgarity and degradation of the tuft-hunter; and from the sullen malignant meanness of the democrat and the republican.' These headmasters wanted power without question and they exercised it vigorously and with almost no check upon their methods. They were concerned with power and influence over the individual mind, the temperament and attitudes of individual boys, the shaping of the boy's intellect, the creation of a man fully competent to serve Church and State. They were earnest and serious in their pursuit, exacting in their demands upon their pupils, setting continuously before their eyes severe standards of learning and conduct. It is easy enough now to deride some of the methods employed, the emotionalism, the appeals to honour, the magnification of venial weakness into mortal sin; it was the very opposite of the permissive society in which some boys now flop and sprawl their way to manhood.

The influence of schoolmasters, especially headmasters, their power over the minds and characters of their pupils, has not grown any less since the turn of the century, though it has over the last fifty years gradually changed direction. When I went to Radley in January, 1915, the war had already begun, and during the war the aims and objects of public schools inevitably changed and were never quite the same afterwards. The rhythm was lost—the VIth form, the university scholarship, the successes in the Schools, the academic prizes, the start upon a professional career—that regular *cursus honorum* was forgotten and in its place the brilliant young men of that age found themselves at the Front before they were 19 and after a few weeks of unquestioning courage in the tragedy of the Somme and in the mud of Passchendaele 'were equal made' with the miner from Durham and the engine-driver from Swindon. Though the war changed many things it did not change the natural ambition which resides in many men to influence and direct the rising generation. Gordon Selwyn, later Dean of Winchester, was Warden of Radley when I went to school. He had been appointed in 1913, at the age of 27, a fact which occasioned some surprise, in spite of the long tradition of young headmasters to which I have referred. Selwyn was a great-grandson of Arnold and his ideas about education were probably not very different. After a brilliant novitiate at Eton and King's, where he carried off with what might have seemed an effortless disdain many of the highest academic distinctions, he was elected to a Fellowhip at Corpus, Cambridge. He was, almost as a matter of course, ordained and was for a time examining Chaplain to the Bishop of London. He accepted the offer of Radley without, I suspect, the smallest reluctance or any misgiving at all, though he had had no experience of schoolmastering. He wanted the power. I have been told that in College at Eton he was inclined to love authority and to exercise a rather high-minded domination over his juniors. Anyone with that stamp of character would clearly be happier as a headmaster than as a don. In his first public speech at Radley he observed that as he had approached the school he had noticed a warning sign 'School. Drive slowly', and this was what he intended to do. His idea of speed did not coincide with the idea held by the Governors, assistant masters and most of the boys. He was precipitate and unwise. His excellent reforms aroused stubborn opposition, not far short of rebellion, and the power which he had desired so much slipped from his grasp. If the school as a whole never fell under his spell but, on the contrary, disliked and derided him, there have been plenty of men, of whom I am one, who have carried about with them throughout their lives the intellectual ideals and the standards of service which Selwyn taught them. He had his peck and power after all and a much more rewarding exercise of it than the discipline which he imposed on the Canons of Winchester, who were, I believe, made to stand up at Chapter meetings and tell him how many attendances at Cathedral services they had kept.

In the post-war years a rather new type of headmaster began to emerge. Classical scholarship and holy orders ceased to be indispensable qualifications for this high office. C. A. Alington, it is true, was in the old tradition. After a brilliant reign at Shrewsbury he had moved on to Eton in 1918. Yet although he was priest and scholar in the usual tradition, his influence throughout the school was wider than, for example, Butler, Kennedy and Moss who had preceded him at Shrewsbury. He was expert at what would now be called 'public relations'. He had, that is to say, a very strong personality, a fine presence and a command of wit not always benevolent. Boys, who had no pretensions to classical scholarship themselves, fell under his spell and remained his devoted disciples and imitators all their lives. He most certainly loved power and he loved the limelight, too, which can be made to play incessantly upon the headmaster of a great school. Public schools in the post-war years needed men of the Alington stamp. Some small public schools founded in the mid-nineteenth century upon the unpractical enthusiasm of Anglo-Catholics or Evangelicals were finding it very hard to keep alive in the post-war world which paid little heed to sectarian principles or prejudice. New and radical ideas about education were in the air and attempts were made to realise these ideas in new foundations; Stowe and Bryanston, for instance, date from these years. There was great competition between the independent schools to attract parents, who after the initial post-war boom found it harder and harder to find the fees. It was necessary then for Governing Bodies to choose as headmasters men who could extend the repute of their schools and attract boys from middle-class families not previously accustomed to sending their sons to public schools. Alington combined this ability with fine scholarship and churchmanship, but it was an unusual combination and one in any case which most schools could not pay for. The priority of choice was for headmasters with boundless enthusiasm for the public school idea—the corporate spirit, the sense of responsibility and service, loyalty and good fellowship—and with expansive personalities and outgoing attitudes. These were the essentials; the scholarship and the holy orders were no longer of the first significance. But these post-war headmasters shared one attribute with their narrower and more formal predecessors—namely a love of power and influence; and indeed I am sure that many men who enter the profession of schoolmastering, especially in boarding schools, have within them as their first choice this desire to influence the young—not to domineer and dominate but to warn, console and guide.

Not all schoolmasters share this ambition. Some of them have entered the profession as a second best. They hoped they were clever enough to be dons, to pursue the particular object of their delight in learning and to hand round, in conditions of undistracted academic concentration, to a group of charming but unpractical devotees the fruits of some rich research into a subject of no obvious significance. There is a disease of learning which infects and debilitates those who are not quite strong enough to resist its onset or to triumph over it. It captivates them, it envelops them, it disqualifies them for positive and practical work. Reluctantly they find themselves turned away from the world of universities because they are not quite good enough and seek to earn their living in what seems at the time the next best thing—a school, an institution dedicated to learning, where the students, or pupils, know, so far, very little, but are anxious, so the imagination suggests, to know much more and to become eager scholars and easy victims to this disease of learning. The two characters who opened this chapter were living evidence that this expectation is an illusion. There are of course some boys who fill the bill, who lap up the distilled wisdom of their learned masters, however ineptly it may be presented to them. But in all secondary boys' schools the percentage must be very small and a learned schoolmaster, if he is to feel satisfied, must have other gifts—sympathy with slow and stupid boys, the art of discipline, which in their hearts all boys hope that their teachers possess, an interest and enthusiasm for games and physical exercises of all sorts, an understanding of boys, their weakness, their sense of humour, their gaiety, their enthusiasms and their occasional torpid and uncooperative moods. If the failed don remains a failed don and can never adapt himself to the probationary level on which so many different types demand attention and assistance, then he will never have any sense of power at all. It is no good sitting, as I remember one of my schoolmasters sitting, with his head in his hands, the class unruly and distracted, muttering to himself in tones loud enough to be overheard that he was the only man on the staff with a first-class degree of the highest quality and that it was a disgrace and a disaster that he should be treated in this way by such ignorant riff-raff. This self-pitying soliloquy was interrupted by the very late arrival of one of the boys in the class, who was stunned and staggered to receive from a man over-strained and overset this blasphemous reproach—'God smash you, boy.' He was not in touch at all.

Other failed dons, on the other hand, were very much in touch. They soon realised the supplementary sympathies required to make them good schoolmasters in their time. I am thinking of one in particular, A. D. James, whose classical scholarship was good enough to make him perceive that to make it any better he would have to sacrifice some of the delight he had in human relationships, in fun and laughter. Instead he used his fine learning to inspire and stimulate into mental activity a VIth form not previously much inclined to see any joy in their work. He himself was alive with enthusiasm for his subject, thinking and talking and arguing, eager, humorous and combative—just as if he himself had been a fifth-century Athenian. The Classical Sixth woke up and gave affectionate attention to their small, dark, vivid mentor, hurrying in and out, sometimes in noisy excitement about some hitherto unobserved poetic effect or some unperceived moment of truth in the history of Athens, and sometimes in a mood of deep despondency, he could not have told you why. But the mood would soon change, and suddenly a dismal inquest into the syntactical shortcomings of his pupils' Greek would be translated into uncontrolled laughter at the attitudes of Falstaff, so that a boy poet wrote of such occasions:

> . . . as when one man
> A classroom and a willing afternoon
> Might be all Falstaff and a Cotswold orchard.

His own sitting-room had an individual welcome for all—for the intellectual boy intent upon an obscure point of scholarship, for the aspiring poet wanting encouragement, for colleagues anxious to be stimulated by his humorous and lively conversation and his lavish draughts of whisky—for everyone except perhaps the over-studious smug swot, wanting to know if his Greek prose had been corrected. It certainly had not. It reposed, with countless uncorrected others, in an indescribable bundle on a shelf above the bed. I do not think that the mainspring of this man's great success as a teacher was a desire for power. He did not think about power. He was young, he was clever, he was gay, he was attractive; he was in love with life and learning and his enthusiasms were infectious. Having come into schoolmastering he made an outstanding success of it. Other men, finding themselves caught up, unwittingly almost, in this exacting profession, coast along, unhurried, undisturbed, indolent and calm, proclaiming that boys' characters are made at home and that advice and interference are acts of supererogation and spiritual pride, excusing their reluctance to embark upon careful explanation and diligent teaching by pompous pretexts about the pervasive value of text books in this 'day and age', so much more potent to persuade and inform than any verbal definitions—which might be provided by a very tired and very idle schoolmaster. It is clear that the love of power and influence is not a part of this man's life.

Such are the non-schoolmasters, who fill up the ranks, as they do in all professions, aimless and nerveless men, who would rather be remote, disengaged and vaguely acquiescent. But there is another type, very different, much more objectionable, but less contemptible—a strongly aggressive type, who love power and wish to exercise it, who become schoolmasters because they can dragoon and bully, not in the higher kinds of society, but among boys, young boys touching the threshold of manhood and anxious to acquire the appropriate steps of entry over it. The type is not engaging but it does not lack significant influence. Charles Lamb has given immortality to one of this type, the Rev. James Boyer, who was the Upper Master at Christ's Hospital at the end of the eighteenth century : —

'. . . J.B. had a heavy hand. I have known him double his knotty fist at a poor trembling child (the maternal milk hardly dry upon his lips) with a "Sirrah, do you presume to set your wits at me." Nothing was more common than to see him make a headlong entry into the schoolroom from his inner recess, or library, and, with turbulent eye, singling out a lad, roar out, "Od's my life, Sirrah", (his favourite adjuration) "I have a great mind to whip you", then, with as sudden a retracting impulse, fling back into his lair—and, after a cooling lapse of some minutes (during which all but the culprit had totally forgotten the context) dive headlong out again, piecing out his imperfect sense, as if it had been some Devil's Litany, with the expletory yell—"*and* I will *too*". In his gentler moods, when the *rabidus furor* was assuaged, he had resort to an ingenious method, peculiar, for what I have heard, to himself, of whipping the boy, and reading the Debates, at the same time; a paragraph, and a lash between; which in those times, when parliamentary oratory was most at a height and flourishing in these realms, was not calculated to impress the patient with a veneration for the diffuse graces of rhetoric.'

The experience of men of my age might almost match this, but not quite. There were still some old and very severe schoolmasters, but the general tendency was towards a more liberal and more sympathetic handling of boys, so that I do not think that anyone of my generation could have written as Lamb wrote and as Coleridge wrote later of J.B., whom he regarded as a very able teacher, a most effective instructor; but when he died this was the uppermost thought in Coleridge's mind, 'Poor J.B.! May all his faults be forgiven; and may he be wafted to bliss by little cherub boys, all head and wings, with no *bottoms* to reproach his sublunary infirmities.'

There was an old man who tried to teach me to sing when I was a small boy at the Junior King's School, Canterbury. If I sang a false note, he advanced upon me shaking his fist and declaiming violently, 'I'll knock your head off, boy.' At first I really believed what he said and I was scared, but when I found that all my friends had already been subjected to this threat many times, that it had always proved empty and that they all thought him eccentric and absurd, I took heart and tried all the harder, I hope, to keep my voice in tune. Everyone will remember the schoolmaster of Sweet Auburn : —

A man severe he was and stern to view;
I knew him well, and every truant knew :
Well had the boding tremblers learn'd to trace
The day's disasters in his morning face.

But on the whole he was gentle, and certainly no overbearing bully :

Yet he was kind, or if severe in aught,
The love he bore to learning was in fault.

He was after all just a simple village schoolmaster far removed from the aggressive Mr Chowlder, ill-rooted in *The Lanchester Tradition,* who 'owed his reputation for strength, not to any breadth of view or depth of sympathetic insight, but to a sublime unconsciousness of his own limitations. Narrow but concentrated, with an aggressive will and a brusque intolerance of all who differed from him, he was a fighter who loved fighting for its own sake and who triumphed through the sheer exhaustion of his enemies . . .' Mr Chowlder has a powerful place in nearly every public school.

Schoolmasters have been fair game for mockery from Holofernes onwards and, though his particular form of pedantry is outdated, there is a tendency amongst many schoolmasters to use the long word, to search for some pedantic or facetious circumlocution—rather in the style of Dickens at his very

105

worst—and I remember a line in, I think, *Young Woodley,*
which carried conviction and admonished me to take care of
my own style. The housemaster breaks in upon a scene of
unorthodox confusion and violence in the prefects' study.
'What is going on here?' he enquires, but immediately recollects
his position and reinterprets his thought, 'What is the significance of this engaging tableau?' This habit of self-parody, the
rather artificial attempt to be witty, to make puns, to score
points by ridicule, to raise a cheap laugh—these are methods of
instruction which can be useful in the classroom but should
never be let out of it. Schoolmasters have always found it difficult to realise that it is much easier to win a reputation for wit
and wisdom among schoolboys than it is among adults. As
Charles Lamb puts it :

> Why are we never quite at our ease in the presence of a
> schoolmaster?—because we are conscious that he is not
> quite at his ease in ours. He is awkward, and out of place,
> in the society of his equals. He comes like Gulliver from
> among his little people, and he cannot fit the stature of his
> understanding to yours . . .

In spite of the new type of headmaster and the new direction
given to public schools since the First World War, this is still
largely true. It is rare, even today, to find a public school master
who is at ease in the world and at home among his equals from
other professions and trades. He is so wholly absorbed, if he
is a good schoolmaster, in the life of the boys around him.
During term-time he lives a twenty-four-hour day in this close
community and even in his generous spells of holiday he is
still inclined to take boys away on walking tours, to visit places
of interest, to organise reading parties and, in these days, to
conduct extensive expeditions in remote countries. Nevertheless a school which is served by several devoted men of this
type is likely to be a very good school. I have known many such
schoolmasters, men dedicated to their vocation, men who
without any doubt exercised immense influence over individual
boys and sometimes over a whole school. These were the latter-
day headmasters, to whom I have referred, who cultivated
public relations in order that they might confer upon as many
boys as possible the acknowledged benefits of a public school
education, with its ideals of service and corporate responsibility.

In May, 1925, Henry Kendall came to be Warden of St Edward's School, Oxford. He was the son of a well-known Liverpool solicitor, and like many sons of professional men in Liverpool he had been sent to school at Shrewsbury. The year was 1903 and C. A. Alington, a sort of prototype of the new-style headmaster, was in charge. He was young, vigorous, inspiring, outstanding among schoolmasters of his time, and Henry Kendall gave him an adolescent devotion which lasted a life-time. In 1909 Kendall left Shrewsbury and went up to Pembroke College, Cambridge, to read History. He was never a scholar, but he picked up at his college a feeling for history, a particular attachment to certain historical characters, an awareness of the large significance of historical events, and a still deeper fondness for academic communities. He was caught, like many men before and since, in the charmed circle of public school and Cambridge and I should think it never entered his head to consider any career other than that of a schoolmaster. But I doubt very much if he was looking forward to the exercise of power when he started to serve his novitiate at the old Grammar School at Bury St Edmunds and at Rossall. He was thinking about friendships, good fellowship, opportunities for service, the civilising influence of books and religion, the corporate life. His delight in these things was greatly increased when he found himself back at Shrewsbury as a master in 1913, back in his dear familiar haunts and amongst his treasured friends. In 1915 he took holy orders, having convinced himself that the Christian religion was the fount of all the goodness and benevolence and delight in living which informed his daily life. He went off to the Navy and served as a Chaplain through three years of war and the wardroom of every ship in which he served very soon came to resemble the common-room of a public school, while the whole ship's company began to understand the cheerfulness and the kindness of the true Christian faith.

When Kendall returned to Shrewsbury in 1919, Alington had been translated to Eton and the Rev. H. A. P. Sawyer reigned in his stead. The selection of Sawyer for one of the most attractive headmasterships in the country was due, not to any particular eminence as scholar or divine, but to his remarkable success as headmaster of St Bees School, Cumberland. This ancient foundation, owing its origin in 1583 to the benefaction of Edmund Grindal, Archbishop of Canterbury in 1575, had for more than three hundred years been providing secondary education at very low cost to the inhabitants of West Cumberland. Sawyer, liberated, as it were, from local obligations by the development of state secondary schools in local government ownership, used the very considerable endowments then at the disposal of the Governors of the school to extend the buildings and to attract boys from a very much wider catchment area; and under his inspiration St Bees was transformed from a good local grammar school into one of the leading public schools of the north. A man who could do this was exactly the man needed by most public schools in the immediate post-war period. Competition was keen and money was short. Sawyer was very welcome at Shrewsbury. He had a great success behind him and his personality was warm and affectionate. He was, in fact, one of the schoolmaster characters of his age, in the public school circle renowned equally for an endearing absence of mind and for an embracing warmth of good will towards everyone within his own circle. Stories of his eccentricities were common currency. Addressing an Old Salopian visiting the school after the war, the headmaster cheerfully enquired, 'Are you you—or your brother who was killed in the war?' Arriving at Shrewsbury railway station to meet a visiting preacher, he quite forgot the object of his presence as the train came in and jumped into it himself, leaving a bewildered cleric in uncomfortable anxiety upon the platform. The stories were legion and Sawyer, who fully perceived their value for his public relations, did nothing to correct or deny them. Kendall learnt from Sawyer the value of surprising eccentricities, the effective exercise of power and control through genial and affectionate manners and, I rather think, a shrewd sense of good finance and good administration. He was very happy at Shrewsbury in this somewhat disordered but strangely effective regimen. He was a housemaster, took an active part in all school activities and was surrounded by many friends amongst boys and masters and warmly encompassed in the embrace of fun and good fellowship. He had considerable influence in his own circle and no doubt he was aware of this, as good schoolmasters are, and enjoyed it, but he was by no means ambitious to seek extended opportunities for its exercise.

St Edward's School, Oxford, founded in 1863 as one of the products of Tractarianism had survived precariously and found itself in 1925 facing an uncertain future. It had no endowment and it experienced great difficulty in attracting boys in sufficient numbers and in paying large enough salaries to keep highly qualified and experienced schoolmasters. But it had had its moments of success and it had turned out into the world a number of men of high quality and promise. In its sixty years of wavering existence it had established a reputation of its own. Anglo-Catholics continued to regard it as one of their educational strongholds and, though the parents of eligible boys who shared this view were few and far between, one or two preparatory schools, notably the Choir School at All Saints, Margaret Street and St Michael's, Tenbury, were eager to supply it with trebles, almost emeriti and of doubtful academic attainments. But this steady stream of musical boys enabled a Warden, who was himself an authority on church music, and a Director of Music of high professional standing to win a wide repute for the school in the musical world. Moreover the school was situated at the gates of Oxford. It was Oxford's public school and, although not very highly regarded in university circles and often not regarded at all, it had acquired from the University a nickname and many generations of undergraduates knew it as 'Teddy's School', that place right up the Woodstock Road where one went sometimes to play rugger and cricket and to hear a pretty good schoolboy concert. The fees had been kept as low as possible in order to be able to offer a public school education to the sons of professional men, notably clergymen with High Church leanings. These are attractive characteristics and anyone who knew the school well at this time liked it very much. But the foundation was narrow, the internal organisation defective, the teaching inadequate and the Governors, and even the Warden himself, had lost confidence in the future. The boys, on the other hand, were very good, good human material, not unacquainted with lawlessness, not scholastically inclined, but bold individuals, striking personalities—Douglas Bader was one of them—waiting and hoping for a bold and adventurous leader. It was at this moment, early in 1925, that the Warden accepted another Headmastership and the Wardenship of St Edward's School, attractive for its proximity to Oxford and its interesting tradition, but ill-paid and with no assured security of tenure, came on the market.

Henry Kendall was roused from his familiar habits, his happy round of work and friendship at Shrewsbury, to think about St Edward's School, of which, being a Cambridge man, he knew next to nothing. He was at last persuaded to forsake all the daily joys of living in a community where relationships were easy and mutual understanding and tolerance not difficult to achieve, to forsake the everyday companionship of his friends, the personal problems and complexities of the young boys in his charge, and to undertake to rule over a school which meant nothing to him at all. It never entered his head that he had been called in to carry out a dangerous, if not impossible, rescue operation. From the first he thought of St Edward's as offering him a wonderful opportunity for the wider dissemination of the good will, the good humour, the cheerful sense of service, which he believed were the mainsprings of Shrewsbury's success. St Edward's was just another school, there were good boys in it, the fees were low and, if the right standards were established and the right facilities offered, more boys could certainly be attracted from professional families. He believed strongly in the public school idea, as it was understood at Shrewsbury and in many other schools forty-odd years ago, and he wanted his school to be the best. If you had asked him what he meant by 'best', he would have brushed the question aside as rather silly and unnecessary. If pressed he would have had recourse to some vague and mumbled definitions—'Best?—well, service, great fun, awfully brave and happy, help each other, no nonsense or pretence, natural, think only of good of school'—each halting phrase preceded by a prelusive murmuring, consisting usually of a protracted letter E, and by a slight turning and shaking of his corporeal frame. The man was dedicated, single-minded, emotionally devoted and that was why he had made a significant impression at Shrewsbury. It required more than buttresses of bonhomie to shore up St Edward's and the effort needed to do this and to expand its influence and success in a remarkable advance quickened in Kendall sources of power, of which he was hardly aware and which he had never thought of tapping.

In a very few years he had acquired immense power within the school, hardly ever disputed and never successfully, and a persuasive influence over his governing body, stimulated and captivated by his exuberant confidence and single-minded devotion. Headmasters of independent boarding schools do, in fact, exercise very great power. There is no question of Cabinet government and collective responsibility. It is wise, of course, to carry your assistant masters with you, but in the end if any of them persevere in dissidence and dissent, you can fire them without reference to anyone else and have some more. As for the boys they must be cared for and cherished and educated. A good headmaster feels his responsibility, in loco parentis, acutely, but here again if one boy proves hopelessly intractable and wild he can be expelled. As for the Governing body, they play no part at all in the daily life of the school and merely have to be informed of expulsions of masters and boys. They have the ultimate say in financial policy, in the policy of development, but, as they are for the most part busy and distinguished men drawn from a variety of professions and living in places far from the school, they are ready enough to listen to the advice of the headmaster and the bursar who live with the problems day in and day out. It is true, of course, that the Governors appoint the headmaster and can, if they so wish, dismiss him. In practice, when a Governing body has so far activated itself as to make an assiduous search for a short list of reputable candidates and then to conduct exacting and difficult interviews, it is most reluctant to repeat the process and only the most grievous and damaging conduct of the school's affairs is likely to make it do so. Some headmasters take great delight in this unfettered power. Theirs is a small world perhaps, but within it they reign supreme and they exercise their absolute authority with complete assurance. Secret cabals and conspiracies are easily defeated and there are no tiresome groups of backbenchers threatening the survival of the Government, and no General Election within five years. They can go ahead with their cherished schemes, the way is clear; and if some of the senior masters wag their grey conservative heads and point admonitory fingers, it is much easier to ignore them than it is for Ministers to ignore senior civil servants, and on the whole much easier to get rid of them. On the other hand, some headmasters find this heavy burden of power and responsibility rather more than they bargained for. They would rather share it, they would rather follow a policy of participation, where masters and boys are too eagerly invited to play too large a part in management. Schools cannot be wholly regulated in this way —or at least not yet—and headmasters who try it are never winners. Kendall came between these two extremes. He had the power and he liked it, but he liked his fellow men more. He had the responsibility and he must run his school. He did not give his power away, but he was human, friendly, humorous, convivial; he must have companions about him and to get them he would listen to their criticisms and their advice with sympathy and understanding, but reserving always to himself, in the last resort, the power of decision. He got his friends and he retained his power. Kendall never married. The school was his wife and indeed its welfare absorbed his every talent and coloured almost every passing thought. Its great success was his reward and the deep affection in which its members held him his only happiness. When he laid down his office after twenty-nine years of incessant activity and unswerving devotion, he received countless tributes of which the following is characteristic :—

I feel very keenly and very personally, the loss to the school in your impending departure. Many fine things have already been spoken in past years about your achievements and these have indeed be_n monumental in physical, spiritual and human qualities. If it is possible, however, I feel that they have all been surpassed by the lasting and profound affection which, unmarred by years of separation, remains for all time between you and those of us who enjoyed the special privilege of having been your pupils, 'sons' and personal friends between the twenties and the fifties.

The exercise of power was never more gratefully acknowledged.

Tributes to schoolmasters fall quite frequently from the lips of those they teach. It is much more common to listen to praise of schoolmasters than to abuse, and if the praise has a touch of amused mockery about it, it is not any less sincere for that. I have seen elderly and retired schoolmasters listening with blank astonishment at words of gratitude and applause from former pupils for instructions and admonishment which had in fact been administered with inward diffidence and self-mistrust. 'You taught me how to row,' I recently heard a very distinguished oarsman say to an elderly schoolmaster whose experience of the art of rowing was severely restricted to say the least of it. But the teaching of oarsmanship takes many forms and the more precise and technical it becomes the less effective it seems to be. I have always heard that the most successful rowing coach Eton ever had achieved his results by running up and down the tow-path in fervent excitement, continuously calling out as he went, 'Try and row better, try and row better.'

I took some pains to discover what some of the great men, mentioned in previous chapters, thought about their school-masters. Winston Churchill, whose career at Harrow was far from glorious, could find expressions of gratitude for some of his. He always had, he tells us in *My Early Life*, the greatest regard for Mr Welldon, the headmaster, and remarks in passing that headmasters have powers at their disposal with which Prime Ministers have never yet been invested. Mr Somervell, who taught English—'he taught it as no one else has ever taught it'—is described as a most delightful man, 'to whom my debt is great'. Mr Somervell then, has his share of praise for the grand Churchillian rhetoric which rallied us in 1940. Winston's success in entering Sandhurst at the third attempt was due—apart from his own 'back-to-the-wall' resolution for which 'no credit was too great'—to the efforts made by a Harrow master, Mr C. H. P. Mayo, who crammed him in mathematics to the point of convincing him that the subject 'was not a hopeless bog of nonsense, and that there were meanings and rhythms behind the comical hieroglyphics.' Asquith, on the other hand, was a natural scholar and probably owed little to the teaching he received at the City of London School, then in Milk Street, Cheapside. He had a great admiration for Edwin Abbott, the headmaster, whom he described as 'a Cambridge scholar of the most finished type in days when that type produced some of its most brilliant specimens.' Abbott himself disclaimed any credit for Asquith's scholastic successes, commenting that 'there was nothing left but to place before him the opportunities of self-education and self-improvement, simply to put the ladder before him and up he went.' Anyone who ever taught a really clever boy would make a similar comment. Harold Macmillan, who won the third scholarship at Eton in 1905, pays tribute to the admirable teaching of Dr Williams at Summerfields. He has little to say of the schoolmasters at Eton. Ill health obliged him to leave prematurely and continue his education with private tutors at home, and during this time A. B. Ramsay, his classical tutor at Eton, came up to London once or twice a week to correct his Latin and Greek compositions. This Macmillan regarded as a 'supreme advantage' and he acknowledges a great debt to Ramsay in every way. In contrast to these three Prime Ministers, Ernie Bevin had very little formal schooling of any kind—nothing beyond the rudiments of reading, writing and arithmetic; while Aneurin Bevan, who left school at the age of 11, hated it and was never interested throughout his life in discussions about education. His view was that boys should educate themselves as he had done.

Wavell was a scholar at Winchester and confesses that he found learning easy, but he was not altogether in sympathy with the Latin and Greek, which were the staple diet, nor with the schoolmasters who tried to feed it to him. It was, for example, never brought home to him that Xenophon was engaged on a 'great historical romance' or that the plays of Sophocles had dramatic and literary qualities far surpassing in interest the textual and syntactical problems which seemed to pre-occupy the attention of his teachers. The headmaster, Dr Fearon, had a high opinion of his ability, '. . . He has a rare gift for scholarship, especially for classical composition; and, if his mind was not set in another direction, he would probably have a brilliant career before him at the university.' M. J. Rendall, the Second Master, was most percipient, writing to Wavell's father, 'I am in all ways satisfied with your boy; both in ability and character; he has a large amount of latent power and all his work is strong. He must be a little more communicative as he grows older.' Although his ability to communicate never showed much advance, the latent power was never, throughout his life, unnoticed by any sensitive person who came into his presence.

Montgomery acknowledges some debt to St Paul's. He was sorry to leave; his years at school had been valuable as his first

114

experience of life in a larger community than home. He had his first taste of leadership and authority and very much relished it, and once he realised that he must work hard he found his masters helpful. He is mildly annoyed by the remarks on his essay writing over the years, ranging from 'very weak' in 1902 to 'pretty fair' in 1906. He claims that now his English is at least clear. 'People may not agree with what I say but at least they know what I am saying,' he argues, adding 'I may be wrong but I claim that I am clear.' I think the schoolmaster who wrote the report on his essays in 1905 was not far off the mark—'Tolerable; his essays are sensible, but he has no notion of style'—and he never acquired one.

It seems to me, as I look back over my varied and erratic experience, that I never exercised more direct power and influence over other human beings than when I was a young schoolmaster at St Edward's School. What is more, I enjoyed it. I enjoyed a sense of positive achievement when I saw dull boys growing brighter, sluggish boys more energetic, arrogant boys more humble, timid boys more confident, solemn boys more frivolous and frivolous boys more solemn. I enjoyed more than anything the friendship which boys gave me, the trust they seemed to repose in me, the attention they paid to my teaching and my advice. In later years I have blushed at memories of my occasional betrayal of this trust, my intemperate use of power, my impatience and my arrogant assumptions. I am continually surprised by the attitude of men, now in their fifties, towards me and my notions of schoolmastering. They will remind me of incidents, in which I employed unjustifiable weapons, wounding invective, excessive chastisement, only to assuage my shame and confusion with expressions of gratitude and no reproach at all. It is very strange and very touching and when these men, themselves widely experienced and mature, seem still to seek out my company and take delight in my conversation, I feel convinced that never in the varied positions which I have occupied since, have I done anything more worth while or felt my existence more justified.

Chapter V

THE UNIVERSITY DON

If the influence of a good schoolmaster on his pupils is direct and intentional, that of a university don is generally much more oblique and haphazard. The pupil is now adult, or nearly so; he no longer needs so much formal restraint and restriction; he is free of constant supervision and correction. He may go his own way, follow his own bent, without much fear of reproof and imposition. Even in 1920, when I went up to Merton College, this was true. The ex-warriors from the First World War found some of the regulations irksome, but those of us who came straight from public schools took infinite delight in a daily régime which offered a rich variety of activities and permitted a wide freedom of choice among them. A slight compulsion began the day with obligatory attendance at chapel or roll call and ended it at midnight with the final closing of the college gate—but between this alpha and omega we employed ourselves much as we pleased and even after the midnight gate was shut we often continued within our collegiate home to wear away the small hours with endless speculation and argument, with close and concentrated study or with immoderate revelry. In the permissive society of today there is still greater licence and to heavy drinking, which was our besetting weakness, have been added sexual promiscuity, drugs and an incomprehensible interest in the policies and the government of the university. To my generation and to many generations after me the dons had no need to strike attitudes of severity. They were our friends and our teachers and only on the rarest occasions our disapproving warders. We laughed at them, imitated them and loved them. Today those dons who take an interest in undergraduates may well be reconsidering their position. Should we, they must be wondering, erect sterner defences around us, retire into a more remote fastness and hand out unsmiling instruction at arm's length? Or should we—as some have already done—make friends with the dissidents and lead the clamour against authority?

If that is one thing which has brought or is bringing a difference of relationship between don and undergraduate, the mania for research into every branch of knowledge, now minutely fragmented, has brought another. I thought the Fellows of Merton, with whom I rubbed shoulders for three years, learnèd to an intimidating degree, but it never occurred to them, I fancy, that the acquisition of more and more knowledge was of greater significance—in their job of being dons—than rubbing shoulders with me and my friends, teaching us, entertaining us and sharing their interests and enthusiasms with us. Most of them did in fact go on quietly amassing learning, adding new learning to old learning, conjecturing and exploring in new fields of knowledge—but without talking very much about it and certainly without sweating and striving to obtain a doctorate which might prove to a superficial world that they were very erudite men. The craze for doctorates had not begun. It was quite enough for a man that he was a Fellow of Merton; no further academic distinction was required. I well remember, thirty-five years later, attending the installation of the Queen Mother as Chancellor of the University of London in the Festival Hall. The occasion was very grand and very splendid. Academic representatives had been invited from every university in the world and most of them were delighted to come—in full panoply, decked out in garish gowns and hoods, each university proclaimed by different colours for each of its degrees, the confusion of colour resembling the coat of Joseph or a Turner sunset, every grave head surmounted by headdresses of outlandish and barbaric design, suitable for Esquimaux or Kurdish cavalry, each garment and each hat weighed down with fur trimmings, the collection of which must have depopulated large areas of Siberia. Elaborate and highly coloured processions were formed at every entrance, each led in by an Academic Registrar, originally appointed, it was clear, for reasons other than ceremonial deportment and each carrying, with an awkward lack of habitual poise, a sort of silver poker lifted clumsily aloft. Among this motley crew peacocking awkwardly along with tail feathers proudly spread, was one solitary figure, spare and sombre, the blackness of his gown relieved only by a touch of glowing red in his hood, and

117

on his head that strange relic of the past, a mortar-board. The distinction of simplicity sat upon him, a grave and reverend Signor, his puritanical black setting at nought the rich splendour of his companions. His humdrum name was A. H. Smith and he was Warden of New College and at that time Vice-Chancellor of Oxford University. Though this does not really illustrate the changed relationship between some dons and undergraduates, the scene has remained vividly with me, emphasising for me the Oxford don's contempt for worldly show and his complete self-assurance in any company, regardless of his exterior trappings. He is an Oxford don and therefore needs no outward or persistent effort at self-assertion. Certainly A. H. Smith belonged to the generation of dons whose early authority coincided with my years at Merton. No doubt there are still many dons with the same ambitions and the same attitudes. But there are other dons at Oxford and Cambridge and far more outside these halls of antiquity, much more interested in their subject, or rather some fragment of their subject, than in their tiresome pupils. I was astonished, when I was taking part in visitations by the University Grants Committee to British universities in the mid-fifties, to hear lecturers complain, not once but many times, that their teaching load was unbearable and unreasonable. How could they be expected, they whined, to keep abreast of their subject, to carry out their much valued research, if they were obliged to do eight hours teaching a week? I had been a schoolmaster in a public school, where twenty-eight hours a week teaching was normal, every other spare moment of the day and some of the night devoted to the service of the boys and thirty-six weeks of them each year compared with twenty-four in the university world. Of course I knew the careers were not really comparable. Profound learning, constantly refreshed, and original work are not expected of schoolmasters. Nevertheless quite a number of schoolmasters have made important contributions to knowledge and to methods of teaching. Others no doubt have remained intellectually idle and obstinately ignorant.

Whatever makes men decide to go in for university teaching —whether it be a simple love of learning or a desire to keep away from the noisy traffic of the world and meditate in peace, 'in desperate sloth, miscalled philosophy'—the motive does not seem to be the desire to exercise any sort of direct power over others or over the policies of the Government. Those men who find eight hours teaching an intolerable burden cannot have any ambition to influence the individuals whom they so seldom and so reluctantly teach. Their ambition is to find out more and more about their chosen subject so that they may be hailed as the acknowledged expert in it. This is a desire more for fame than for power. But scientific research may lead to unimaginable positions of power, where the deliberate destrution of the world becomes a practical possibility. Rutherford, himself a powerful personality, was searching in his Cambridge experiments for the release of superhuman power, but he had no wish to have any power of decision about its use; and nobody who knew the late John Cockcroft could have seen in this gentle and lovable man an insatiable lust for power. He exercised a great deal of power all the same, both during and after the war, the power which comes inevitably into the hands of a man, whose comprehension of the practical applications of scientific experiment and discovery goes far beyond that of most of his colleagues. The use of atomic energy for widespread destruction disturbed him profoundly and he was insistent to his dying day that its proper use was for the progress and prosperity of mankind. The aim of scientific researchers is to unlock the closely guarded secrets of the nature of the universe and of human life, to find out who we are and why we are, but not to exercise any form of power over us.

Historical and literary research has much less obvious aims and not often any very practical application. It is a delightful pastime all the same and if a piece of research results in, for example, a fresh, original and revealing biography of a great historical figure, it can be extremely influential on the minds and thinking of certain types of men. Too often, I fear, this sort of research leads almost nowhere. I have heard scholars admitting that they found the research itself absorbing and exciting, but that when it was finished the effort of communicating it, of writing it up and publishing it was just a bore. Sometimes they do not even attempt it; a wonderful piece of forgotten knowledge has been discovered and it remains locked up in the discoverer's head and dies again with him. Sometimes scholars will force themselves to publish what they have with such delightful pains unearthed, and the result is unreadable. 'They make a solitude, and call it research' my old tutor used to say, adapting Tacitus, but he was an old-style Oxford don. H. W. Garrod could have passed for nothing else—the affectations of manner, the weak and quavering drawl, the shy, self-deprecating air strangely at variance with the confident opinion and the combative assertion, the impish wit ever on the alert to deflate all forms of pomp and pretence, an appetite for learning which made him a polymath, but with constant sympathy for and understanding of lesser minds which genuinely pursued knowledge and taste and style; these disciples he embraced and cherished as all great professionals do. When Garrod became a don, first at Corpus in 1902, and then at Merton in 1904, power was the last factor in his consideration. He was very clever and by Oxford standards this really means something out of the way; and I do not suppose he pondered long before deciding to continue the quest for classical learning so that he might hand it on to others, by becoming a don. This was his natural progression, further researches into the texts of Latin and Greek authors and the teaching of Honour Moderations to young men following the well-worn route to success. In the ten years between coming to Merton and the outbreak of war in 1914 the fruits of his researches were seen in editions of Statius and the second book of Manilius' Astronomica and in the revision of Wickham's Text of Horace. He was pleased, I have no doubt, with these performances, but he cannot have felt the full satisfaction which comes from the exercise of all one's powers. He has shown that he had the power to edit Latin texts—not entirely to the satisfaction of A. E. Housman, it is true—but at least as well as the other leading Latinists of his time. It was a limited sort of power and a limited sort of fame and as Garrod advanced in life he was not without a taste for the latter. His teaching load at Merton was not a load at all because it was this which brought him his first contacts with the undergraduates in the College. He found—rather to his surprise I suspect—that young men liked him and indeed as time went on his personal magnetism was very strong and his rooms became a sort of friendly and hospitable common-room of Garrod's friends. Here was power of a different kind—the power to influence the attitudes of young men, to stimulate their intellectual and artistic interests. He never analysed it to himself in this way and indeed he never made any deliberate or premeditated attempt to correct and improve, as a school-master does. 'In the back of my mind,' he once wrote, 'there lies always the suspicion that the love of literature, like that of virtue, is probably best taught in asides.' It was in fact in this way that he taught us both.

The war came and at the age of 36 Garrod found himself transplanted from the happy and not altogether difficult routine of life at Merton to a position first in the Ministry of Munitions and ultimately in the Ministry of Reconstruction. He became, that is to say, an administrative class civil servant. Many dons had this experience in 1939 and both they and the Service profited from it. The same can be said of Garrod in the First War. He was good at the job; his intellectual powers were capable of anything. His duties brought him into contact with a much wider and much rougher world than Oxford. When I went to live in West Cumberland in 1936 his recollections of that remote area were stirred. He had been sent there to take part in some industrial negotiations and he had an abiding picture in his mind of tough West Cumbrian iron ore miners, obstinate and difficult and by no means prone to give a warm welcome to the gentlemen from Whitehall with their clever ways and fancy accents. He went to the United States with C. W. Bowerman and J. H. Thomas to discuss labour relations in war and found himself making patriotic public speeches in Middle Western cities about Britain's war effort—a very unexpected assignment for an Oxford don with a weak speaking voice. But he was a great success. He did it very well and proved to be a popular orator. His American audiences had certainly never seen or heard anything like him before. He had discussions with President Wilson himself :

There was a memorable day
I talked with Wilson, and before
Many days passed one day more
I talked with Wilson. That was worth
Leaving the other end of earth.

These experiences had, I have no doubt, a strong effect upon Garrod's sympathies and his ambitions. It is characteristic of him that he never allowed the hard intellectual grind—whether it were tough negotiation or the editing of Statius—to drive the poetry out of him; and his verses quoted above are concluded thus :

> One night the moon rose, and I got
> Her midmonth splendour as she shot
> Out of the black Potomac, right
> On Washington's Column, and her light
> Laved with wan glory that grave might
> Of granite, that bare greatness well
> Figuring his, the unchallengeable
> Supreme American. I wonder why
> Just that moon and that memory
> Linger, so very loth to die?

If the varied and exacting work of a civil servant in war-time enlarged Garrod's knowledge of the world and his intellectual scope, the tragedy of the war 'humanised his soul'. Garrod loved his friends; he always loved his friends. He lost many in that first war. His sense of bereavement was so strong that he sought relief by bitter words about the men who came back to Merton after it :

> I hate your chatter overhead,
> And your jests that fall like lead
> Where only golden things were said
> By the men that are dead, the men that are dead.

That was a short-lived mood and one or two poems in the same vein were a 'timely utterance' to give relief to his sense of loss.

Garrod came back to Merton after the war a more powerful personality, his feelings deepened by suffering, his intellectual energies widened by experience—the experience, for example, of dealing with 'the general economic problems created by a world shortage of capital, supply, tonnage, etc'. So well did he handle these difficult problems, as remote from the text of Horace as the sun is from the earth, that his superiors in the Civil Service described him as 'a man of quite exceptional ability and of more than academic distinction'; and obtained for him a C.B.E. He did not know he was more powerful; I suppose he never thought about power. But he found it hard, I fancy, to take refuge from the practicalities of life, its problems, its griefs and its joys, in Latin scholarship. He might have become, if he had been so minded, the Corpus Professor I daresay, but he turned aside to English literature and concentrated his gifts on Wordsworth and Keats and other English poets, and continuously extended his human contacts, his circle of devoted disciples and friends. He did not abandon learning. He was as learned in the English poets as he had been in the Latin, but he wanted a closer embrace, a warmer colour, than he could get from authors some 2000 years dead. He occupied the Oxford Chair of Poetry from 1923-28 and thereafter went to Harvard for a year as Charles Eliot Norton Professor. Apart from this visit to America he lived in Merton until he died in 1960, occupying his time with a considerable amount of critical work in English literature—notably his edition of Keats in the Oxford English Texts—and a serious excursion into Renaissance scholarship for the benefit of his friends and much industrious research and learning devoted to his College. This is not the path of power; but the conduct of his life, the expansive generosity of his temperament, his kindness to his friends, his affection for them, his fastidious taste, his contempt for the cheap and shallow, the abundance of his wit and humour—all these and many individual oddities of manner, many lightly held prejudices, made up a personality of such magnetic power that men, themselves of great ability and independence of character, turned first to him in moments of intellectual or moral perplexity, sought his advice, drew strength from the sources of his knowledge, and then went about their daily tasks, renewed and fortified, and acting often, though they hardly knew it, as his faithful disciples. When he died, it seemed to many of us that the College died with him and we could scarcely bear to walk across Fellows' Quad in sight of his windows or to climb the staircase which had so constantly led our willing footsteps to his door. Teatime or the interval between tea and dinner were good times to find him. Over the tea-table there might be a few young men, toasting the buns or offering the tea, the room lively with silliness and banter, the solemn rows of books which occupied the wall space confined to a learned aloofness in this hour of levity, the available table space piled high with books and papers currently in use, the old typewriter momentarily silent and disused, the old typewriter where Garrod habitually tapped out his letters and his scripts in a form and fashion only slightly less illegible than his handwriting. The room seemed overfull— a large room, with two windows overlooking the meadows to the south and two fronting the neat Jacobean elegance of Fellows' Quad. When the 'boys' had gone he would sometimes, if he felt in the mood, press you to stay on, and there reclining upon his sofa, quietly puffing a cigar and twirling his eyebrows, he would shyly open, for your delight, his treasure-house of knowledge, taste and opinion. His range and scope were very wide and like Dr Johnson, with whom I always thought he had some affinity, he talked with wise authority and as effectively on practical subjects of the workaday world as on learned themes.

I have not been describing an ordinary man or an ordinary don. We were lucky in a way in which many Oxford men— and Cambridge men too, no doubt—have been disappointed, looking for guidance and example which they did not find, hoping for sympathy which they did not receive, contenting themselves in the end with mockery, a surprised mockery at the eccentricities of their dons. Wordsworth wrote this of the Fellows of St John's College Cambridge in 1789, and it has not lost its force nearly two hundred years later :—

With playful zest of fancy did we note
(How could we less?) the manners and the ways
Of those who lived distinguished by the badge
Of good or ill report; or those with whom
By frame of academic discipline
We were perforce connected, men whose sway
And known authority of office served
To set our minds on edge, and did no more.
Nor wanted we rich pastime of this kind,
Found everywhere, but chiefly in the ring
Of the grave Elders, men unscoured, grotesque
In character, tricked out like aged trees
Which through the lapse of their infirmity
Give ready place to any random seed
That chooses to be reared upon their trunks.

Th attitudes of undergraduates to their 'grave Elders, men unscoured, grotesque in character', did not change much between 1789 and 1920 and has probably not changed much since. The Warden of Merton in my time was a byword for meanness, a miserly recluse, who lived in a vast gloomy house in Merton Street, entertained nobody, rarely entered his College except to attend a College meeting, to preside at end-of-term Collections, or to cast a chilling shadow over Sunday Evensong, when he sat darkling, brooding and scowling in his stall, staring with implacable hostility at the devout under-graduates beneath him. New College men still boasted of their Spooner and attributed to him all kinds of speech inversions which he certainly never made. Magdalen men were careful to have respectable grandfathers to satisfy the snobbish scrutiny of President Warren. The Head of one famous House was alleged on his ninetieth birthday to have ordered a new suit of clothes with two pairs of trousers. Apart from Heads of Houses, who perhaps attracted the most universal mocking surprise, there were many other dons in all faculties and all Colleges whose voice and demeanour filled the young men with incredulous amazement. How could such creatures be? For example, could Dr Grundy, of Corpus, really be taken seriously? The Corpus men thought not, and Merton men, who wanted to learn from his lectures on ancient history, soon found their wish unfulfilled, because a claque of Corpus men at the back of the room found his simplest sentence, his most ordinary precepts, a cause for such abandoned hilarity that the lectures were rendered largely inaudible and wholly incom-prehensible. We loved them all, we imitated them, we invented stories about them, but I fear we did not hold them in high respect. They had no power over us and I do not think that worried them in the least. They were not interested in that sort of power, nor most of them, I should guess, in any sort of power at all.

There are plenty of these learned ineffectuals and elderly grotesques still haunting universities, caring little for the learn-ing they profess and nothing for the young men to whom they try to teach it. There is no bitterness in this opinion : after all I was very lucky, Garrod was my tutor and our imitations of him were certainly the sincerest form of flattery. Besides, the Oxford system—and, in fact, every university teaching system in this country—is designed to teach a man how to work alone.

Working alone was to most of us a novel experience; working alone, not for one or two hours a day, but for the whole working week, less the six or seven hours spent at tutorials and lectures. This was a test of intellect and character. Were our critical powers of mind and our habits of meditation strong enough to make our study productive and to enable us to resist the hourly and delectable temptations to 'good-natured lounging'? Working alone is not easy for the young. It seems chilly and friendless until you begin to realise that the books on your shelves—'the spirit breathed from dead men to their kind'—are your faithful and loyal companions, not, as some living men are, personally critical and accusatory, but full of experience and wisdom, anxious only that you should share, in tranquillity, the knowledge and the feeling that are between their boards. The habit, begun perforce at Oxford and not easily acquired, grows upon a man as he seeks refuge from the daily traffic of the world's business and the insistent clamour of its rude disputation. The middle-aged man of affairs looks back with envy to the 'oak' which he so seldom and so reluctantly 'sported' against his darling friends.

Between Garrod, to me and many of my friends a unique human being, and these non-dons, these rather ludicrous figures, there was, and is, a large number of very competent men, scholarly and industrious, sound teachers and temperamentally sympathetic with the ignorance and aspirations of young men. Such men exert power, no doubt, insensibly spreading around themselves a personal influence; but that is not their motive and they do not think of their job in those terms. Outside this number, however, are men who seek power of a different kind. There have always been dons at Oxford and Cambridge to whom politicians and public servants would turn for objective advice. Dr Jowett, for example, renowned Master of Balliol (1870-93), had considerable influence over the form of examination to be administered to candidates for entry into the Civil Service after the Northcote/Trevelyan Report in 1854. In my own lifetime H. A. L. Fisher, a prominent academic and later Warden of New College, was called in by Lloyd George to be Minister of Education in 1916. John Maynard Keynes moved from King's College, Cambridge, and the Bloomsbury group into the Treasury in 1915 and his radical ideas on economics immediately began to make an impact. In 1919 he went to Paris as principal Treasury representative at the Peace Conference. He saw much which he distrusted but was unable to prevent. At the end of the year he published *The Economic Consequences of the Peace*—a brilliant and bitter attack upon the principal peacemakers and in particular upon President Wilson. There was perhaps some injustice, and more than a touch of arrogance, in the virulent criticisms by a young academic economist of a man who had been President of the United States for seven years and knew a good deal more about the restricting confines within which political power can be exercised than Keynes ever did. The attack was characteristic, however, of the polemical methods employed by academic disputants. Keynes had not forgotten that Wilson had started life as an academic and had proceeded from the Presidency of Princeton to the Governorship of New Jersey and thence to the White House.

The last Labour Government, in this country, although headed by someone who was originally an academic economist, showed itself eager to call to its assistance from both the ancient Universities, regardless of nationality, self-confident economists who imagine, I suppose, that the practical economists in the Treasury are much less competent to deal with our national discontents than they are. It is hard to believe that this is the case and indeed there is no proof that it is. Nevertheless an interchange between the public service and the academic world is healthy for both. In the last war a strong stream of academics flowed into the Civil Service and at the end of the war flowed back again. They brought with them into the direct service of the Government intellectual qualities of a very high order and the habit of forming objective judgments after a silent, careful and scholarly sifting of evidence. They carried back with them, to the benefit of their colleges and universities, orderly notions of hard practical administration. This was in fact an involuntary change of direction for these men and women, brought about by war-time needs and the war-time powers of the Minister of Labour. It was not the result of a sudden longing amongst dons for power in the policy-making machine. Some of them liked the change very much and were soon exhibiting remarkable talents as administrators and policy

127

advisers. Their careers have been outstanding in their generation. Lord Franks, for example, left the pursuit of economics at Queen's College, Oxford, to become a civil servant. In a few years he was Permanent Secretary in the Ministry of Supply. At the end of the war his college reclaimed him as its Head, but after two years in that comparative tranquillity he was sent off to Washington as British Ambassador. From that most glittering and prominent assignment he took a quite different turning and presided for eight years over Lloyds Bank, but he could not resist the magnetic charm of his origins and now reigns in the Provost's Lodgings at Worcester College. In the course of occupying these very high positions he has also performed much public service as chairman or member of many Committees of Enquiry on a large number of different subjects. It would be very interesting to know which of his jobs gave him the fullest sense of power.

Hardly less enterprising and varied is the career of Lord Redcliffe-Maud. He started as a philosophy don at University College, Oxford, in the thirties, young, enthusiastic, influential with the young men. Just before the war he accepted the Mastership of Birkbeck College in the University of London, the working man's college, as it was then called, as different in every respect from University College as Moscow is from Paris. The war then diverted him into the Civil Service, where he made his mark in the Ministry of Food. He was persuaded to stay on in the public service and he occupied with distinction first the Permanent Secretaryship of the Ministry of Education and then that of the Ministry of Power. That was not enough and now he must deploy his extraordinary gifts as High Commissioner in South Africa and subsequently, after South Africa left the Commonwealth, as our first Ambassador. But, as with Lord Franks, the charm of Oxford still held him and he returned as Master of the College where he was a young don. Again like Lord Franks he has served and is still, as I write, serving on Public Committees of Enquiry and Royal Commissions. Where has he found the fullest sense of power?

I would cite two more such unusual and important careers. Lord Murray of Newhaven, educated at Edinburgh University and Oriel in agricultural economics, found himself a Fellow and Bursar of Lincoln College, Oxford. The war sent him to the Middle East where he was Director of Food and Agriculture at the Middle East Supply Centre from 1942 to 1945. Before he had been released from these war-time duties the Fellows of Lincoln had elected him their Rector and he returned to a most enviable job, the job of renewing an old and small college after a world conflagration. He did it so effectively and made such a name for himself that in 1953 he was induced to leave his College and become Chairman of the University Grants Committee, a position of enormous responsibility, exacting, onerous, and offering intermittent power and influence over higher education in this country, intermittent because he did not hold the purse-strings, and what he and his Committee wanted to see done was often frustrated by the Chancellor's preoccupation with priorities which he thought more pressing and more important. After ten years in this sensitive and difficult position, Lord Murray moved into the world of industry, and is now a director of the British Aeroplane Company.

Lastly comes Sir John Wolfenden, the traditional Greats man, moving at the age of 27 from a Fellowship at Magdalen to the Headmastership of Uppingham, getting his first taste of Whitehall during the war when he spent some years as Director of Pre-entry Training at the Air Ministry. In 1944 he left Uppingham to be Headmaster of Shrewsbury and six years later moved into university administration as Vice-Chancellor of Reading. In 1962 he succeeded Murray as Chairman of the University Grants Committee and now, very much against the book, is the Director of the British Museum.

These are four of the great all-rounders of our time, who have exercised power and authority in many fields. They are all friends of mine and I would not dream of analysing their motives in moving so famously outside the normal gradations of a single career. They provide proof of the value of the highly-developed all-rounders in the conduct of the nation's affairs. Not one of them could have imagined, or indeed hoped, on the day when he was first elected to a Fellowship that this was the first step in a career of change and variety and bringing with it wide responsibilities, advisory and administrative, and far-reaching power and influence over men and organisations. But for the war, most of this would probably not have happened. In the world of science and technology there is a close link between universities and Government. Even in peace-time universities will undertake scientific research which Government cannot find a place for in its own research establishments and Professors of Engineering are well accustomed to act as consultants to local and central Government from time to time. In war very large numbers of scientists and engineers move into the direct service of Government and many of the inventions, both defensive and destructive, which have increased the efficiency of our armed forces can be attributed to them. The informed scientific intelligence and skilful advocacy of Sir Henry Tizard were responsible for the earliest possible use of scientific inventions—notably radar—which saved this country from destruction in 1940. Throughout the war Lord Cherwell sat at Winston's elbow, whispering sour doubts and saturnine criticisms into his strangely receptive ear. He was far from always being right in his opinions; his predictions were often falsified and his tactics generally unscrupulous, but he brought to all disputes and discussions, to all planning, a very jagged edge of thought. He was sardonic, he was contemptuous. No mutual admiration society could ever flourish under his baleful eye; and in very close and secret circles this is important.

In recent times it has become fashionable to summon political economists into direct Government service in the hope that academic theory will prove more efficacious than practical experience in curing our chronic economic disease. Royal commissions and public committees of enquiry have never been without academic members, bringing from all kinds of universities the fruits of deep objective thinking on particular subjects. They have their influence. They can make inroads into the settled complacency of practical operators and that is very important : but where the inroads develop into the rout of the practical operators the result is very dangerous. Conclusions based on bright ideas, untested and untried, are even worse than the stodgy and unimaginative conclusions of some experienced professional administrators.

But these summonses of university dons to public service are haphazard and unpremeditated. Most dons certainly have no secret hope at the time of their election that one day they will be able, through some unforeseen circumstances, to exercise power over national events and the men taking part in them. It will be a very sad and sorry day for education in this country when clever young men choose university teaching as a stepping stone to political or administrative power. It is, however, their continuing duty to obey the summons to public service when it comes—just as Garrod did in the First War and my four all-rounders in the Second.

One of the great figures of my time at Oxford was Walter Raleigh and he, it is certain, entered upon his career as a university teacher with no thought in his head about the exercise of power over men or events. He believed that his own education had contributed a great deal to his natural zest for living. Life was given to you to be enjoyed and the proper study of English literature helped you to that end. Successively he occupied Chairs at Liverpool, Glasgow and Oxford and his lectures, often ill-prepared and formless, but always lively, gay and brilliantly coloured by his own imaginative love for great writers and great writing, drew enthusiastic crowds of young men and women who gathered from his lips a stimulating taste for life and learning. He had, in fact, a great uplifting influence over these young minds and in his last years, when the war had seemed to take a lot of the significance out of learned research, his interests centred more and more upon the personalities and the human problems of the men he taught and the men in whose company he passed his life. Indeed this had always been his mainspring—his love of men and their God-like qualities and his distrust of formalised programmes of education and dull, stereotyped methods of teaching. He would have had a lot of sympathy with some of the reasons for the present student unrest in this country and surely he would have known how to handle it. In a letter to John Sampson, dated New Year's Eve, 1904, he writes:

'Tell Mackay to stop founding universities. There's no sense in them. Bottled men, gone putrid, that's all. And they spread like mould on cheese. If a university or two would bust up, or resolve itself into an Agapemone, my spirits would go up. Damn the education of the young, anyhow. They're too good to be fouled this way.'

If he had lived another forty or fifty years he would have seen his wish come true, but, though he would have applauded the objections of students to dull matter dully delivered and to neglect and inattention on the part of their dons, he would, I think, have poured lively scorn upon the claims of students to a voice in the government of the university, while their preoccupation with national and international politics and their exhibitionist methods would have moved him to anger. That was not the business of young students. He himself was not interested in politics and certainly not in party politics. He was knighted in 1911 on the joint recommendation of Asquith, the Prime Minister, and Balfour, the Leader of the Opposition —just about the only point of agreement, I should guess, between these two men in that year of bitter political controversy. He was, however, absorbed by the imperial achievements of Englishmen. He was inspired, all his life, by a strong spirit of adventure. He always talked with enthusiastic warmth about Elizabethan adventurers and his own book, *English Voyagers,* was one of his favourites. The war stirred these impulses still further and Raleigh was delighted when he was asked in July 1918 to write the official history of the Royal Air Force. He was full of praise for the backroom historians and researchers who worked for him, if sometimes astounded by their voluminous diligence. In response to a request by him for a brief and concise piece of research, they presented a very long and highly elaborated document. At the sight of this he made a remark, which Winston himself would not have disdained, 'I asked for cream and you bring me a cow.' He had just finished the first volume when he flew out to Baghdad and Mosul on 16 March, 1922, to see for himself, as it were. He returned on 25 April, with typhoid fever and died in Oxford on 13 May, 1922.

His untimely death—he was only 60—was much bewailed by devoted colleagues, friends and admirers from many colleges and many walks of life. 'Beyond dispute' Garrod wrote after his death, 'Walter Raleigh was one of the great figures of the Oxford of his time. Nature had made him for a notable man in any society.' And then he goes on to speak of his towering figure—he was 6ft 6 in tall—his nobly-shaped and finely-poised head, his long, lean and mobile face, his uniquely brilliant qualities of mind and his great social charm. His death cast a gloom over Merton and although most of us had had, in the nature of things, very little direct contact with him we had been very much aware of his presence among us. His appearance alone marked him out as a king among men, and to hear him speak, to be with him in a room, to pass him in the quad, was to feel instinctively a brilliant radiation of life and laughter coming out of nim. When suddenly this vital splendour was miserably extinguished the whole college felt a blast of grief and dismay. His coffin was brought to the college on the eve of his funeral and placed in the chapel before the altar. At whose instigation I know not, it was decided that a vigil should be kept throughout the night and some of us took it in turns to stand alone for two hours in the dimly-lit chancel beside his coffin. To young and sensitive feelings this was a lonely, awesome and difficult experience. The weight of a vast antiquity lay upon us, the darkness and space relieved only by the light of a few candles casting shadows into the dim recesses of this splendid building. But to me, looking back on it from 50 years later, it was one of those clearly remembered times, not infrequent in life, when the occasion seemed to demand an elevated concentration of thought and feeling of which the mind and heart were pitiably incapable. The next day the chapel was packed, as I had never seen it before, with his relations and friends and admirers to pay him homage at his funeral service. 'The funeral service in Merton College Chapel is unforgettable,' wrote David Nichol Smith—unforgettable because it seemed so appropriate to pay a last tribute to an unusually fine spirit in a building of such immense and beautiful proportions, a building which had for centuries witnessed the prayers and praises of generations of those young and enthusiastic Englishmen, who appealed so much to Raleigh. The college had no professional choir, but the undergraduate choir did its best and the vast congregation joined in the familiar hymns which Lady Raleigh had chosen. After the service many numbers of the congregation went in specially hired buses to Ferry Hinksey for the committal. It so happened that two or three of my friends and I travelled in one of these buses with Robert Bridges, the Poet Laureate. The additional emotion which this unexpected proximity produced in us was soon transmuted when this confident bard complained in loud tones to those

133

around him that the College should have provided much more impressive music for the funeral service. It was terrible and shameful, he declared, to insult a fastidious spirit like Raleigh with such hackneyed and worthless hymns. We were hot in our defence, boldly disclaiming any responsibility on the part of the College for the choice of the hymns. Our protestations were roughly brushed aside. As Wordsworth wrote, 'The poet, gentle creature as he is, hath like the lover his unruly times.'

The power of men like Raleigh and Garrod and of many others no less notable is never sought and is indirectly and obliquely exercised. Their power is over the minds and attitudes of other men and its exercise is imperceptible and unpremeditated. When they are called by circumstances and fate to involve themselves in public affairs they manage very well because their minds are finely-tuned instruments, but I should doubt very much if the power of administrators is as deep and effective as the power of good dons and good schoolmasters. In a free society it is the men who count, their processes of thought, their sensibilities, their touch and their taste. Men are the victims, in some degree, of their heredity, and they are subjected to many influences, the conditions of their homes, the personalities of their parents and other members of their families, then to their schoolmasters and their dons; and the sum of these influences produces the man who goes out to work in the world. Yet a good many university teachers with deep stores of learning, sensitive taste and lively sympathy with the young, are often diverted to the disputatious world of university government. They must serve on this committee and on that committee, they must be free to argue and speak their minds on administrative as well as academic matters. They are suspicious that somehow or other lay administrators are too stupid to understand and handle academic administrative problems; they regard them in any case as failed academics and treat them as below the salt. For some university teachers this is a delight; it gives them a sense of direct power, which they have failed to realise in their dealings with undergraduates. For others it is a rather disagreeable chore of duty; it takes them away from their beloved research and their stimulating contact with the young. In colleges at Oxford and Cambridge the Fellows govern themselves. The financial resources of a college, and its financial problems, may be very large—the problems larger still if the money is short—but even the largest college is not a university and the time spent on its government makes no severe inroads into the time left for teaching and research. It could make even less if dons placed more trust in lay administrators and did not feel that they alone could manage what are to them abstruse and controversial subjects. Dons make these things harder than they need because being factious by tradition they feel it important, and a sign of their individual superiority, to oppose every solution which they have not devised.

The comparatively light burden of administrative duty at Oxford was one of the reasons why Raleigh was tempted away from Glasgow. 'I had to choose,' he writes, 'whether I would take a chance of being a man of letters, or become a university politician and a popular preacher.' He chose to be a man of letters and in making that choice became at the same time, not so much a popular preacher, as a lively and liberalising influence over the hundreds of undergraduates who thronged to his lectures and over the minds and manners of his colleagues.

In his time the Senior Common Room at Merton included men of formidable intellectual power. F. H. Bradley, though he lived in remote regions of thought, was a real presence among us. H. C. Wyld would have been a prosy lexicographer without the irresistible stimulus of Raleigh's conversation and sense of fun, while David Nichol Smith, exact, painstaking and devoted scholar, blossomed into a wise humanity of opinion and judgment in the daily comradeship of Garrod and Raleigh. This is the collegiate life, founded in mediaeval concepts of Christianity, by the revolution of the ages extending its embrace to secular activities, the pursuit of disinterested learning, and the liberal education of the young. And to the young and sensitive what an education it seemed, an education which many of us would happily have continued over a number of years.

The most obvious and the ultimate power of dons would, in the opinion of many, be their power as examiners, their power to confer or withhold a degree, and to arrange the candidates for degrees in three or four classes, to elevate a man as first class or to degrade him as third. This branding is thought to have great and enduring significance. The world will still pay an awed respect to a man who thirty or forty years earlier was awarded first class honours in the History School at Oxford, even though he has long ceased to care anything about history or any other branch of learning and never reads anything more spiritually profound than the *Economist* or a Government White Paper. The third class man will struggle all his life to explain away this offensive label and dons themselves will be very slow to forget or forgive it. 'It seems to me incredible,' I heard a don saying to a member of the College, aged 60 and considerably distinguished in the world, who had just made a brilliant after-dinner speech at the College Gaudy, 'quite incredible that a man who got a third in Honour Mods should be able to stand up and make the kind of speech you would expect from an Ex-President of the Union with a first in Greats.' Incredible to him, because to him Honour Moderations and the like were the ultimate and decisive test of a man's ability, he knew nothing else. Most dons would not take this narrow view. They would disclaim any ability to predict a man's future career when they were awarding him a class. All they were doing, they would say, was making a careful and professional judgment about the strength or weakness of a man's answers to a set of questions, carefully designed to test his knowledge and his critical faculty, on a restricted group of allied academic subjects on successive days in a particular month in a particular year—no more than that. Moreover they could not know, or take account of, the mental and physical condition of the candidate at the moment when he was writing his answers to their questions. Napoleon, it is often alleged, lost the battle of Waterloo because he had a headache. And what was the physical and emotional state of A. E. Housman, when he failed outright in the final examination of Literae Humaniores at Oxford? It must have been a temporary disturbance, since after translation to Cambridge he became the most learned English Latin scholar since Bentley. A friend of mine used to confide in me, when he was very slightly and attractively bemused with alcohol, that his whole career would have been altered if he had not lunched in Queen's in the middle of his Honour Mods. He had lunched extremely well, as men do in Queen's when time and money are no object. He had lunched with his friends and he was very happy and very relaxed as he picked his bibulous way across the High to the Examination Schools. In flushed and sanguine mood he answered with unusual self-assurance the questions the examiners had put to him on the writings of Lucretius about the nature of things. He had always been confident about this particular special book. He had assiduously attended Cyril Bailey's excellent lectures. He knew the text well and the subject had roused his critical interest. Here was an undoubted alpha and his confidence in this result received no check as he wrote with light-hearted abandon through the three hours of that March afternoon. But in the tragic end the examiners could award nothing better than a beta minus and this wretched mark had dragged him down from the second to the third class. He could be right, and if he had scored the expected alpha and achieved a second, his career might well have been quite different—and not nearly so varied and interesting. Raleigh consoled his more wayward disciples with the unorthodox opinion that the prig sat in the first class, the ordinary man in the second, while the poet sat in the third class and laughed. He was himself living evidence that the dictum had no universal application; for he had achieved a second in history at Cambridge and nobody would have dreamed of calling him an ordinary man. But Raleigh understood clearly the real and limited significance of classified degrees and used constantly to remind his pupils that first degree examinations and the Day of Judgment were two examinations and not one.

Nevertheless the power of examiners is real and for all their protestations and disclaimers their judgments can affect the careers of those they examine. It works both ways. For one reason or another the good scholar has a succession of off days. He is stale, he is nervous, he is tense, stretched to breaking point by the terrible consequences which may flow from his pen. He flounders miserably, and the examiners, some of whom are certainly aware of his true merit, have no option but to suppress their inner conviction and their compassion and award him the class which his disordered answers deserve. Another man, continuously disappointing in his weekly work and his collections, convinced by the lamentations of his tutors and their gloomy predictions that anything better than a third is beyond him, will march into the Schools, with nothing to lose, not much worried by thoughts of what is considered sound and orthodox and what is not, and will write with the spontaneous flow of a liberated spirit. Here and there the examiners will detect a touch of original brilliance and a long viva with the young man, completely relaxed and unafraid, will convince them that for all its falterings here is a first class mind.

The clamour for examination reform is constant. The long written examination is not a fair test; there are too many incalculable factors at work. The examination by group tests and extended interviews is weighted in favour of the outwardly self-confident man and against the deeply thoughtful scholarly type who is timid in his approach to others—and so on. No form of examination invented by men can be absolutely reliable. Examiners are well aware of this and in most cases their mistaken judgments weigh heavy on their consciences. But they most fervently wish that the world would not attach a significance to these judgments which was never intended and is dangerously misplaced. Examiners—university dons—do not love this power. Most of them exercise it with humility and reluctance, praying, as all men pray, that the Disposer Supreme and Judge of the Earth has, unlike earthly examiners, found an infallible and compassionate method of testing us frail and frightened human beings.

Chapter VI

THE REBEL

Professor H. C. Wyld, the Merton lexicographer, to whom I have already made reference, defined a rebel as '(a) a person who openly opposes and flouts lawful authority, especially one who offers forcible resistance to lawful government—(b) a person impatient of, opposed to, control or constraint of specified kind.' Oliver Cromwell, I suppose, starts his public life in the first category, but ends it vigorously defending what he considered 'lawful government' against rebels of a different colour. The wheel had come full circle. Of the men I have discussed in this book none, I think, comes in this first category, but several, at the start of their lives or at some time or other in their lives, have found themselves in the second. It could even be argued that, in political life at any rate, the most dynamic, the most successful, leaders have all tasted the strong wine of rebellion but at some point short of intoxication have turned aside to a steadier and more sustaining vintage.

Churchill spent a good deal of his political life in rebellion of one kind or another. In the First World War his dangerous initiatives alienated both Liberals and Conservatives, and before the war was over he found himself anathema to both. Moreover the mighty and invincible party, which in the years before the war supported in power a Government as active and effective as any in our history, was tearing itself in pieces. Loyalties were hopelessly divided between Asquith and Lloyd George whose temperaments were for ever incompatible and whose notions of personal conduct in both public and private life differed far more than Fox ever differed from Pitt. Between these irreconcilable forces the Liberal Party withered away. Its decline was perhaps inevitable—the eclipse of a centre party dimmed and extinguished by the rising constellation on its left and the settled luminary on its right. But the decline was hastened by this tragic clash of human personalities.

By 1925, then, Churchill was discredited and the party he might have led was on the verge of ruin. From these disappointed hopes Stanley Baldwin rescued him and for a few years he was prominent, though not universally approved, as Chancellor of the Exchequer. The rebellious mood returned and, out of office once again, he belaboured the Government for its Indian policy, its neglect of defence and its pursuit of appeasement in Europe. There were many men, in the 1930s, who felt that he would be well advised to give up politics and devote himself to authorship. They could see no future for him. The Cassandra voice grew tiresome, especially when it was raised in a rather futile and unpopular defence of Edward VIII. He seemed too eager to oppose everything, to be a rebel for rebellion's sake. He would never, it was widely felt, command enough confidence and support to sit in No. 10. But the war, which he had so boldly prophesied, gave the lie to all these timid forecasts and there is no doubt that his method of conducting that war, his flow of ideas, his critical probings, his restless refusal to accept unwelcome advice and his oratorical powers had been sharpened and heightened by his courageous years of hammering and hacking at the apparently monolithic structure of an insensitive Government with a huge majority.

By contrast Neville Chamberlain was never much attracted by the flavour of dissent. Within the principles of his own party he was a conformist, a good administrator and a steady reformer. He had been an unusually constructive Minister of Health and might have been an effective Prime Minister, if he had not been lured away from the familiar path of domestic affairs by the rise of Hitler and Mussolini into the, to him, unknown and unexplored labyrinth of international affairs. His temperament was assured and self-confident. He found it difficult to believe that he could be mistaken even on subjects which were new to him. He did not possess the divine spark of leadership which sets alight the courage of a nation fighting to survive and he was incapable of that surge of indignation and revolt which carries ordinary men and women to acts of heroism and sacrifice. He kept a tight control over himself, dominated his colleagues and the House of Commons with his intellectual superiority, but never stirred the emotions and affections of the people.

Stanley Baldwin was in a different class, that enigmatic company in which perhaps Attlee, a very different type of personality, might be classified. The only revolt Baldwin ever led was against his King and the object of that manoeuvre was to preserve order, stability and established authority. Attlee presided over the preliminaries of the evolution of the Empire into a Commonwealth, but his object also was preservation and not upheaval. Both were intensely patriotic, loving and cherishing English attitudes and English customs, but neither could have led the country in war. Nor for that matter, I believe, could Ramsay Macdonald. He seemed, as I have said, to many men the fervent and uncontrolled apostle of revolution. In fact he was nothing of the kind and it was only the fact that he actively embraced pacifism in the First War which made men think so. His humble beginnings and early struggles against penury had led him inevitably to the adoption of socialist principles and membership of the Labour Party. He was one of the most active and eloquent of the early leaders of the movement. But he married into an upper-middle-class family, whose intellectual and artistic interests and social customs he found far more congenial to his own temperament than the harsh cries and rough actions of the *sans culottes*. There was no sudden conversion in 1931. It was not the deep persuasive tones of the old King's voice, nor the blandishments of duchesses, which induced him to lead a national Government pledged to protect the pound sterling and uphold the Establishment. It was in a sense the natural climax of his career, as it was also the beginning of his end.

Aneurin Bevan was a dedicated rebel, a man to whom rebellion and dissent were, I should guess, more attractive and more seductive than office. He knew both. He laid the foundations of the National Health Service, he accepted the Ministry of Labour with a seat in the Cabinet, but was not really unhappy, I suspect, at finding a pretext to resign. He had been a good Minister, good in the sense that he pushed his own ideas and was never content to accept the official view, the school solution, without relentless inquisition. He was a good Minister in another sense. He was full of ideas, eloquent, imaginative, exuberant, but always attentive, considerate, and humorous. Civil servants could, and did, disagree violently with his opinions and his ideas, but they were never made to feel like schoolboy upstarts, advancing careful and considered views, yet summarily dismissed, derided and ignored, as if they belonged to a mean and mercenary class. Nye Bevan was friendly and convivial with all sorts and conditions of men, but only if they responded and did not sit stultified by prejudice and orthodoxy. He entered Parliament in 1929, representing Ebbw Vale, a South Wales mining constituency. There was everything in his own circumstances and in the conditions in which his friends lived, everything in his own temperament and in the attitudes of remote and superior persons who knew nothing about the lives and struggles of miners, whether dangerously employed or not employed at all, everything inside him and everything he saw in the Podsnaps facing him, to turn him into a rebel, fiery, importunate, remorseless, unwilling to compromise or to be reconciled with those hard-faced men in both parties who failed to deal with the problems of mass unemployment, failed even to understand them and sometimes even refused to recognise their existence. His own party disowned him, the Tories feared and shunned him. Successive Prime Ministers were the targets of his scorn, Chamberlain for his obstinate complacency, Churchill for his conduct of the war. To Churchill he seemed, in the war years, 'a merchant of discourtesy' and 'a squalid nuisance'. He had to oppose, he had to rebel, he had to provoke—the best contribution he could make, he felt, to the conduct of a war in which he played no executive part. Like all true rebels he found loyalty to a leader very difficult to achieve. Attlee was a constant target for his invective and even after the war when Bevan served in Attlee's Cabinet he was never an easy bedfellow. Attlee, who, as I have said, thought government should be organised on the same lines as a good regiment or a public school, must have slept easier when this boisterous and hot-headed boy voluntarily left the school.

Gaitskell also suffered from his temperamental disloyalty. All rebels have it. It seems to be a fixed principle of their nature, so that the true rebel must always defect, disobey and disagree, unless he is called upon to occupy the highest place himself. Then he develops all his powers and realises his perhaps unspoken ambition to lead and not to follow. Lloyd George did not rest till he had pushed Asquith out of No. 10 and Churchill had never inspired great confidence in colleagues or the public until the war. It always seemed to me, as it did to many others, that the Labour Party made a great mistake when they elected Gaitskell as their leader instead of Bevan. Gaitskell was by no means 'the desiccated calculating machine' that Bevan once called him, but his intellectual integrity and his deep sincerities were not enough to inspire wide popular support and his somewhat austere devotion to the cause made it hard for him to understand, let alone control, his exuberant and unpredictable second-in-command. If their roles had been reversed, the Labour Party would have been formidable indeed.

To my great regret I never knew Nye Bevan. I saw him from time to time at meetings of the Cabinet or Cabinet Committees, exchanged perhaps an official word or two, but never enjoyed any personal contacts or relished his unbuttoned conversation. He was a controversial figure, hated and loved in equal degrees. His famous 'vermin' speech made him many enemies. It was ill-judged and unjust. There is vermin in all political parties. The phrase was by no means new in political warfare. Wordsworth, an early rebel too, speaks of the British Government in the 1790s as—

Giants in their impiety alone,
But, in their weapons and their warfare, base
As vermin working out of reach . . .

When I came to work as an Under-Secretary in the Cabinet Office in 1950 I got a different insight into Bevan, this many-coloured man, when he was Minister of Health. I was entitled, in accordance with the rigid system of class privilege in the Civil Service, to have one large or two small pictures in my room. I went across to the Ministry of Works to make my choice. I peered around in their subterranean gallery, moving with dissatisfaction and discontent from one portrait of George II to another and from one Landseer to another. At last I espied some very exact and very delicate Chinese water colours of flowers and butterflies, exquisite workmanship carefully and deliberately insulated from any background and any association with the world of men. Nothing, I thought, could be less appropriate to the walls of a room in the tumultuous Cabinet Office and nothing more soothing and more curative to its harassed occupant. I chose two, my maximum allotment. The set, I was told, had been bought recently in a sale in an attempt to satisfy the artistic requirements, emotionally defined, of the Minister of Health; he had been satisfied and there were six of them hanging in his room.

By contrast Anthony Eden was never a rebel, and could never have been a rebel. It is true that deep convictions and personal pride obliged him to resign from Chamberlain's Government. He became a sort of rebel for the first time. We applauded and hoped that at last the powerful combination of Churchill and Eden and other bitter opponents of appeasement might defeat Chamberlain or at least deflect him from his pitiable and dangerous self-assurance. But Eden missed his chance, or perhaps never attempted to seize it. 'If Eden had been big enough,' wrote Nye Bevan at the time, 'he could have ruined Chamberlain.' Instead his resignation speech was flat and insipid. The opportunity went by. The fact was he had no stomach for rebellion. It was not his *métier*. He preferred power and influence and adulation, the plaudits of international crowds, the congratulations of royalty and prominent persons. Nye Bevan judged him harshly, calling him 'the juvenile lead' and adding, 'he is more pathetic than sinister. He is utterly outmatched by his international opponents. Beneath the sophistication of his appearance and manner he has all the unplumbable stupidities and unawareness of his class and type.' That is severe and by no means fair. It is the voice of a born rebel raised in scorn against a very talented man who had nothing to rebel about. When in the tragic decline of Eden's career, he stiffened the sinews and summoned up the blood and bravely, and many thought most unwisely, determined to obliterate Nasser he was not quite equal to the task. The long years of elegance and conformity had sapped his strength and his stamina.

Harold Macmillan, brought up in the same 'class and type', was of a different mettle. When he rebelled he meant it. He took a firm and unwavering stand against the policy of appeasement and he was a rebel too over economic policies. He was the member for Stockton-on-Tees and he saw at first hand what unemployment really meant. It was not just trends and curves and lines on a graph. It was men and women in tragic personal distress, no money, no work, no prospects, no hope, nothing for them and nothing for their children but penury and idleness stretching on, as far as they could see, from generation to generation, world without merciful end. He was deeply moved and he rebelled against the faint-hearted efforts made by successive Governments to remedy this dreadful disgrace. Some prominent politicians secretly believed that there was no cure, that nothing could be done, and that, if a free capitalist society was to survive, this appalling sacrifice of human life and happiness was inevitable. Macmillan found such a view totally unacceptable and he was one of the first Tories to preach the revolutionary doctrine of a mixed economy and some measure of State interference to prevent this degradation of man.

I never met Macmillan at this time, but I saw the same problem in the north-west, in West Cumberland, where the incidence of unemployment was quite as bad as it was in the north-east—35% of the insured population. I knew about this. In 1938 I became the so-called District Commissioner for the Special Area of West Cumberland—a grandiose title for the Government official charged with the duty of initiating and supporting schemes for the rehabilitation of the area and of introducing new industries. The duty was honourable and onerous but for its performance the Government had given these Special Area Commissioners very limited powers. The ultimate control was exercised as usual by the Treasury in London and with John Simon occupying the Chancellor's chair there was not a lot of confidence and hope in the stricken areas that these Commissioners would be given the chance of making much headway. Nevertheless local machinery had been set up and in each area there was a Development Council, consisting of prominent local representatives from both sides of industry, from local Government, from banks, insurance, etc. These Councils had the task of promoting surveys of resources, schemes for economic improvement, the development of amenities—anything in fact which might contribute to the attraction of new industry into the area and to the introduction of more trade and more money. The District Commissioner naturally attended all meetings of the Development Council and in West Cumberland he and the Secretary of the Council shared an office building; evidently the two men must work hand in glove if there were to be any worthwhile results. It was

145

here I met the rebel of rebels—my beloved rebel, John Jackson Adams.

Jack Adams came from an iron ore mining family in West Cumberland, the youngest of nine sons in a family of thirteen. His father, whose weekly wage was twenty shillings, was killed in a mining accident when Jack was four years old. Jack received a short and perfunctory education at the Arlecdon Elementary School and then at the age of fourteen went to work in the mines himself. It was very tough going, a long walk in all weathers to the pit-head, a day of dangerous and heavy work in the unnatural and unwholesome atmosphere of an iron ore mine and the long trudge home, repeated day after day, very little money or comfort, and the constant threat of unemployment hanging like a sword of Damocles. As he grew up in these grim and straitened circumstances he saw a lot to criticise in management and was acutely conscious of social injustice and bitter inequalities. Unlike Anthony Eden, he found much to rebel about. It was not surprising that he became an ardent disciple of Keir Hardie. It was no pacifist tendency which made him an active opponent of our participation in the 1914-18 war, but a fiery mistrust of authority, a conviction that it was a capitalists' war for the exploitation of the working man. He naturally interested himself in trade union matters and being a man of powerful physique and violent feelings, with a tongue of unlettered but natural eloquence, he soon came to be regarded as a dangerous hot-head. Employers fought shy of him. He was always looking for trouble, and he approached them with a rude and arrogant self-confidence which alarmed and alienated them. He took a prominent part in local politics, becoming a County Councillor in 1922 and later Chairman of the County Health Committee. After the passing of the Special Areas Act in 1931, some very far-sighted person, by a miracle of persuasion, managed to argue Jack Adams into accepting the Secretaryship of the Development Council.

In 1938 I came and worked in the room below him at 30 Roper Street, Whitehaven—a house typical of the town at that time, once a prosperous and elegant private residence built in the local red sandstone, now, like many houses around it, remarkable only for its air of crumbling decay. I came from a very different and rather narrow professional world. I knew

146

very little about the conduct of Government business, still less about industry, trade unions and local Government. I learned quickly in a rough school. In my first days as I sat in my room listening with patience and attention to the calm and reasonable arguments of my Civil Service deputy, I was continuously conscious of a dynamic commotion in the room above. Often the commotion reached a sort of climax, the clamour of voices and the stamping of feet increased and suddenly there would be an unceremonious irruption into my room of a squat, square, swarthy figure, stamping and shouting in a broad West Cumbrian accent about the duplicity and incompetence of the Commissioner's Department. At first I was a little frightened of him. He talked very fast and very violently. In discussion of our problems he used every weapon of invective that came to hand without any respect whatever for the feelings of his antagonist. He seemed full of hatred, of anger and mistrust. At almost the first meeting after my arrival there was a violent altercation between several different interests—employers, trade union leaders, Government officials and so on—and one man in particular, with repeated accusations and abuse, roused the implacable anger of Jack Adams who at last shouted across the table in tones of unmistakable purpose, 'If you say that again, I'll tear your bloody liver out.'

For all the violence of his criticism, his uncompromising attacks upon me and my kind, I very soon began to admire the penetration of his mental processes, the sensitive energy of his feelings and the restless activity of his whole being. I admired all that—it was impossible not to—but I began to love him too. He could be very hostile and very aggressive, offensive in the extreme, but only against the one particular point of your performance which had roused his wrath; he did not include the whole of you in his contempt and fury. Very soon I became aware of the deeply affectionate side of his nature. He could blast you and deride you—it was the privilege of his job—but if any extraneous person tried to do the same that man's 'bloody liver' was not secure in its place. Jack was logical when it suited him, pursuing his logic to the utmost, but he would quickly throw it all aside to defend his friends on whose behalf he would marshal all sorts of illogical but telling and forceful arguments. It is impossible to say of him, as it is of most of us

147

I suppose, why he loved some people and hated others, but it is quite certain that in the violence of his feelings he did not allow much interspace between the extremes of love and hate; yet although he might be abusive he was also compassionate. Like most men of highly charged emotions and dynamic energy, he could, as could Churchill, be easily moved to tears.

His mind was restless, forever questing and probing, never accepting 'no' without a strenuous battle. He was brimful of ideas, some of them quite unrealistic; but he would never admit it without a protracted display of angry pugnacity. When clearly beaten in argument he would never accept defeat, but would charge away at once upon a quite different subject. The flow of words was torrential—a Canadian visitor amongst us once remarked that he had heard nothing like it since his visit to Niagara—the accent obstinately West Cumbrian; for a new-comer like me the combination of speed and accent made comprehension difficult. It was no good asking him to repeat, it was no good making any interjection. He simply did not listen but pursued his own multifarious lines of thought, addressing himself to nobody in particular but determined to hold on to the end. When the end seemed to have come, we were too stunned and breathless ourselves to offer any useful observations before he was off again on some different theme. I used to wonder how he had managed to acquire such an encyclopaedic knowledge of the district, its industries, its agriculture, its customs, its history, its social facilities, its personalities, everything indeed about it. How did he acquire it considering he never seemed to listen to anyone or to spend much time in silent reading? Indeed silence is the last thing that the memory connects with Jack.

He was my guide in every sense. We went everywhere together. We went to inspect disused sites still available for new industries, where old industries had once flourished, where there was ample floor space, good connections by road and by railway sidings, plentiful labour at the very door, but now cold, empty and forgotten. We tramped together over new sites, specially and carefully chosen for their natural and factitious advantages, where we might build up-to-date factories and let them to industrial tenants with new and developing techniques, refugees, perhaps, from the Nazi terror which now overshadowed the whole of Central Europe. We visited local authorities, cajoling them with grants, persuading them by one means or another to improve and extend their services, water and sewerage and the rest, so that new industries might not be deterred by the lack of them. We went to Carlisle to enlist the support of the County Council officials. We went to London to interview prospective tenants for our empty factories, old and new—tenants of all types and nationalities, Austrians, Greeks, German Jews, Englishmen seeking new outlets for investment or greater security from the war-time bombs which would inevitably descend upon the south-east of England. We addressed Rotary Clubs from Barrow to the Border, we were guests at Chambers of Commerce dinners and made speeches of encouragement and hope. We set in hand plans to clear the waste lands of industrial failure and obliterate the scars of exploitation. We attended countless meetings. There were frequent meetings of the West Cumberland Development Council, with Major Hibbert in the chair, but largely dominated by Jack, the Secretary. He suffered from none of the modest and self-deprecating attitudes of traditional committee secretaries. His report occupied a large part of the proceedings. Criticisms of the Council's activities were answered by him in terms of the utmost pugnacity. Constructive suggestions were accepted with little outward grace or gratitude, not seldom as ideas which had occurred to him months before and had been discarded as irrelevant or unrealistic. This was the manner, ungracious perhaps and egotistic, but nobody could fail to be aware that in him was the source of power and action, the single devotion to the cause. He might boast and bully but nobody could match his dynamic enthusiasm and his range of ideas.

At meetings of the West Cumberland Industrial Development Company his manner was different. This was our Trading Estate Company with powers to build and let factories to industrialists, who were not able or willing to lock up capital in bricks and mortar. The Chairman of this company was Robert Crichton, a wise and experienced Scot, who after years of skilful and energetic service to the steel industry had taken on this difficult but inwardly rewarding task. We were all most attentive to his opinion. He knew far more than any of us about the economic facts of industry. Where we were naively enthusiastic about some half-baked scheme for bringing employment to large parts of West Cumberland, he was realistic, practical, but never hard or unsympathetic. This combination of practical sense and compassionate sensibility commanded the respect and affection of Jack, the restless and indignant rebel, and of me, the zealous amateur. At meetings Jack might start in rebellious hostility to the selfish claims of capitalists or the niggardly attitude of the Government, but with patience and tact and experience Crichton would bring him to a more reasonable and constructive frame of mind. Jack honoured him and deferred to him; and I cannot now recall any other man about whom I could say that—except Professor Daysh of King's, Newcastle, who did a remarkable survey of West Cumberland and took an abiding interest in its problems.

Of all our Councils and Committees the West Cumberland Industrial Development Company was the most practical and most constructive. On the ground, on the Solway Estate at Maryport, at Cleator, at Hensingham, at Distington, you could see the fruit of its labours—men and women at work again, taking home with their pay-packet pride and satisfaction and hope. We came to think that nothing else mattered; if we could convert pointless indolence and frustrated energy into a regular job of work, even if it were uneconomic by national standards, we had gained a victory for humanity. We had translated doorstep disgrace and disenchantment into the dignity of daily work and due reward. We had, of course, our failures, industries which we had induced with concessions over rent and rates and so on to the limit of what we were allowed to offer, but which never managed to establish themselves and capture an economic market. But we had our successes too, industries which repaid our early nurture with healthy increase and handsome profits. Perhaps the most glittering of these successes is to be seen at the Hensingham Silk Mills near Whitehaven. The Chairman of this concern is now a figure of national regard, a leader in his profession, and a smiling, friendly patron of artistic endeavours in the north. He, in fact, combines in himself the sensitive percipience of the artist and the hard practical sense of the industrialist. But nobody knew this when he first came to this country in the thirties—nobody, that is, except Jack Adams, who, employing his personal and exceedingly selective radar, seemed at once to detect unusual quality and distinction in this man, who found himself immediately the object of Jack's affectionate solicitude.

Sometimes Jack and I made visits to London to interview prospective tenants of our factories, to embark on a negotiation with them, to assess the soundness of their financial position and the likelihood of their success. Jack was always eloquent in praise of West Cumberland, its resources, its facilities, its amenities and above all its plentiful supply of skilled and unskilled labour. No question ever floored him. Whether he knew the answer or not, statistics and information poured out of him like a torrent, which no interruption could stem. The questioner became bemused and awe-stricken and if in his confusion he seemed to express any doubt or anxiety about the suitability of West Cumberland for his particular industry he was very soon put in his place, and if he persisted in his hesitations written off altogether. If on the other hand he made a favourable impression on Jack, if he listened attentively and seemed eager to come, then he was at once taken up, brought into the fold and given promises and expectations, sometimes rash and overpitched. In all cases Crichton cast a very critical eye on the proposals we put to him and if he and the other directors found any of them risky and unsound we had to back down and disappoint an enthusiastic client. But for the most part Jack's judgment was pretty good and he was more likely to err in severity than in leniency.

Our visits to London were usually brief. We were too busy to stay long. We would take the night train from Carlisle one night, stay one night in London perhaps, and come back by the night train on the next. This gave us time to enjoy some good meals and a few drinks. Jack was no Puritan. He enjoyed eating and drinking. He would push his way into some quite expensive restaurant, loudly demanding a table, blowing rank smoke incessantly from an overworked pipe, complaining sharply at what seemed to him any lack of attention. The menu was of little interest to him. The French names meant nothing. 'Do you speak French?' I once politely asked him. 'Of course not,' he shouted, 'can't speak my own bloody language.'

151

Anyway he was almost certain to want steak and beer or whisky; he didn't go much on wines. He enjoyed all this and did his utmost to make you enjoy it too, most lavish and generous if he were the host, convivial and high-spirited, telling story after story with unrestrained gusto, his lack of conventional decorum a striking Cumbrian commentary on the dull postures of respectable Londoners. His uninhibited manners were a great delight to me and once I remember the rich patrons of the Carlton Grill startled into curiosity by his excited behaviour. He and I had been involved all the morning in an important negotiation with an old-established Yorkshire firm who were thinking of making a considerable expansion in West Cumberland. This would mean a very acceptable slice of employment and we were most anxious that the negotiation should succeed. I had an ace in my hand in the shape of the rent inducement which I was allowed to offer and I fancied I was playing my cards most cunningly by holding this ace back to the last. Indeed I was always under instructions from my Department not to play it at all if I could help it. But Jack on the other hand was always, and especially on this occasion, nudging me and whispering in my ear and urging me to get on and show the card. At last I did show it and the bargain was forthwith clinched. The directors of the firm generously invited us to the Carlton Grill and there with great jubilation we celebrated our agreement. It was not surprising that the modish clientele were staggered by Jack's elation. This was without any question at all something which Crichton would—and did— approve.

We were making some solid progress, though not enough and not quickly enough, when the outbreak of war changed everything. The natural resources of our area, which it was uneconomic to tap in peace-time, became invaluable to a country about to be subjected to a vigorous blockade and which would in any case have to cut its imports to the barest essentials. Surplus manpower, which had for so long been an embarrassment, in a moment became the nation's most priceless asset. The Government, which had previously tried to minimise the problem, to make the numbers of unemployed appear less than they really were, was happy now to maximise this great reservoir of manpower and to proclaim the advantage of this powerful reserve. It seemed to us, who had laboured together in hope and faith, a cynical commentary on the conduct of human affairs that men were valued only when they could be offered as a sacrifice to the god of war. To Jack, I think, the outbreak of war brought feelings of bitterness and doubt. His constant aim, his most cherished hope, over the past years, had been the economic recovery of West Cumberland and with it the return of personal prosperity, happiness and dignity to all its inhabitants. Now the exigencies of war might bring economic recovery but only at the expense of violent partings, shattered homes, wanton destruction. He was a radical, even a revolutionary, but he was constructive, he believed in progress and in the benign effects of the spread of education. He honoured learned men, perhaps because he himself had received so little formal education, and he devoted much of his time to the work of the County Education Committee and the governing of White-haven Grammar School. Now, once again, education would be no more than the prelude to slaughter.

With the outbreak of war the active work of the Special Areas Commissioners was over and after some frustrating weeks I was withdrawn to other duties. I had been hand in glove with Jack for just over a year and, though I saw him inter-mittently both during and after the war, that exciting and rewarding partnership was broken. I used sometimes to think that the full processes of school and university education would have turned him into one of the outstanding Englishmen of his time. But I wonder. Not seldom, education can be a taming of spontaneous impulses, a blunting of the sharp sword of an uncontrolled spirit, the exchange of a grand ruggedness for a smooth veneer. Jack, I believe, was better without it—violent as a restless windswept sea, uncurbed, ungovernable; stilled sometimes and suddenly, like that sea, to calm and compassion so that he seemed at such moments 'even the gentlest of all gentle things'. Later in life his matchless contribution to the recovery of West Cumberland was widely recognised and rewarded with a Peerage. 'Lord Madams' he would brusquely announce himself, but to me he was always Jack.

In modern times each of the great political parties gives uneasy asylum to a brilliantly difficult rebel. On the left Mr Michael Foot exerts his vitriolic charm. He seems cast in the role of James Maxton. His tongue is a scourge and everybody loves him. At times he seems to despise his own leaders far more than his political opponents; and certainly he prefers rebels of any colour to the grey conformists. His sting is sharp and sudden, but he does not press it home. Even the *Times* leader-writer cannot resist two columns of affectionate praise; and I can remember hearing Winston Churchill, himself a one-time member of the rebels' league, rounding upon an unfriendly and complaining colleague with some annoyance— 'Why? What have you got against him?' The secret is, perhaps, that Mr Foot is at heart a hero-worshipper—in politics Aneurin Bevan, in literature Hazlitt, and hero-worshippers are nearly always loveable men.

On the right, the wild eyes of Mr Enoch Powell survey a scene which brings him no joy and little hope. Yet if he fails to please his leaders he speaks for many thousands of his countrymen on topics about which their passionate feelings are in tune with his; and he speaks, as they cannot speak, in learned phrases, marshalled in lucid order, and set on fire with fervid rhetoric. He is, I think, entitled to feel some grievance against his leaders who raise no voice of protest at the vile obscenities with which their political opponents assail him. The pollsters and psephologists can analyse and argue for ever; the deciding factor in the 1970 general election may well have been the fact that Mr Powell was a member of the Conservative Party, that Mr Powell was brilliant, brave and patriotic and that 'that very silly man', Mr Wedgwood Benn, had smeared him with guttersnipe calumny. But Mr Powell is likely to remain a rebel, a dangerous and uncomfortable misfit in his party, just as Churchill was before the last war. He shares many things with the rebel Churchill, the upsetting gift of prophecy, a command of rhetoric, though of a different style, and a weakness for chasing too many hares at one time. Men who follow Powell on immigration and the Common Market find his rather hysterical accusations against those prim and bloodless Home Office civil servants so far-fetched as to be derisory; and that brings all his judgments into doubt.

I know neither of these men. Mr Powell I have met a couple of times and enjoyed with much relish a few minutes of penetrating conversation. When I lived in Eaton Terrace I used occasionally to see him in the street taking his daughter to school. Mr Benn would not understand why I treasure that little memory. Mr Foot I have never met. But I have read his first volume on Nye Bevan; he has reproved me for rash opinions about relations between Wordsworth and Hazlitt in the correspondence columns of the *Times Literary Supplement* and I have heard him lecture on Hazlitt. That is how I know he is a hero-worshipper.

There are men of naturally rebellious temper in the Civil Service and in the fighting Services, but evidently as the authority of the State rests upon these public servants rebellion amongst them does not earn extensive promotion. There is an occasional Curragh Incident, sometimes a strong protest and resignation on grounds of conscientious disagreement with Government policy. There were many sensitive public servants whose consciences were tormented at the time of Suez, but in general the public service is a disciplined force with an obligation to obey and uphold the Government. In consequence civil servants—I am speaking again of the Administrative Class —are generally considered to be orthodox, conformist, authoritarian and rather dull. This is often the picture which they present to the outside world, some of them because they have been stifled with convention and some to hide the awkward anguish of their contempt and disagreement. To most men Normanbrook appeared cold and conventional, the springs of spontaneous feeling dried up, any flicker of rebellion in his heart long since extinguished. He was much more interesting than that. His mind was a fine instrument, his judgment sensitive and discriminating. From time to time he regarded Government policies, whichever party was in power, with contempt, and in private he adopted the language of rebellion. I believe that as a very young man he was not unattracted by unorthodox attitudes and ideas, but his utter devotion to duty, as I have already described, drove him into the posture of a supremely effective engine-driver, determined on one thing alone—to hasten the train of Government along its appointed track without deviation or accident.

Military men are in much the same boat. They are tied by oath to the Government they serve and their obedience must follow the recognised chain of command. They may blast off in the mess or the wardroom against the treacheries of Governments and the crazy incompetence of senior officers, but, if they are going to stay in the fighting services, in the open they must toe the line. Hence most of them become the type of their own Service, rigid and blinkered, professionally self-confident, inflexibly attached to orthodox opinions and school solutions, often impatient and ignorant. But behind the steady blue eyes of that assured naval officer, behind the firm mouth and clipped assertions of that arrogant soldier, behind the rather more relaxed manners and lazy acquiescence of the R.A.F. officer, there sometimes lurk impulsive and rebellious thoughts. If these impulses become too tumultuous or too obsessive, there are stops and starts, doubts and resignations. Others who survive their fury of dissent may write a book or two just this side of revolt, and still go on to high command. In practical methods these men are rebellious, in principle they conform. This might be said of Montgomery, in respect of personal appearance and public relations, and of de Gaulle, whose revolutionary and radical views on the conduct of warfare did not prevent him from becoming the Chauvinist Emperor of France. During both world wars, there were a number of fighting men such as T. E. Lawrence and Orde Wingate who believed that they had discovered warlike tactics of decisive originality. They were not unmoved, I sometimes think, by the conviction that their ideas were quite outside and beyond the orthodox thinking of their professional superiors. It is, however, an important commentary on the whole question of military orthodoxy and originality that the two Generals most sympathetic to novel methods and untried tactics were Allenby and Wavell, quite wrongly regarded by many as the pattern of steady and uninspiring generalship.

I was a witness to the feelings of deep discontent and mistrust with which men view what they think the plodding action of an over-trained and orthodox military machine against a different kind of enemy in very different circumstances. It was felt in many quarters that the deployment of several British battalions, conventionally trained and used on a tactical system devised in the Second World War, was quite inappropriate for subduing the considerable bands of hirsute ruffians who lived in small marauding groups in the limitless forests of the

Aberdares and Mount Kenya. The Mau Mau leaders were glad to dignify themselves with the resounding ranks of the British Army, but their tactics were in no way like those of the admirable British General who opposed them. The critics were even more severe about the operations conducted by the R.A.F. which sent out squadrons of aged Lincolns on bombing sorties against area targets in these same forests. The local joke was that the Mau Mau welcomed these air raids. It was easy for them, enjoying such a wealth of natural cover, to evade the bombs. The wild animals, however, had no prescience in these matters and buffalo occasionally slaughtered by these haphazard affairs enabled the Mau Mau to sustain their strength with unexpected and plentiful feasts!

As usual in circumstances where amateurs freely criticise professionals, the amateurs were often wrong, but they certainly had a point or two and in the spokesman of their many discontents I met another notable rebel. Michael Blundell was a farmer in the Subukia Valley, living in a comfortable house surrounded by a garden of the most profuse loveliness. The Mau Mau rebellion was a shock and an affront to him and many like him, who treated their native labour with generosity and compassion. Blundell had been a Member of the Legislative Council since 1948 and in 1952 became the Leader of the European Members, so that when the rebellion began it fell to him to voice the angry doubts of the Europeans about the conduct of operations and their mistrust of the ability of the orthodox Government machine to deal with the crisis. Changes were introduced and Blundell agreed to join the Emergency War Council, which was in fact the effective instrument for conducting the war. The Governor, Sir Evelyn Baring, was the Chairman and the other members were Sir Frederick Crawford, the Deputy Governor, and General Sir George Erskine, the Commander-in-Chief. I was the Secretary. I felt at first that Blundell considered that his only duty was to oppose and complain. His objections were numerous and vigorously sustained in lengthy periods of emotional invective. I found his somewhat strident and undisciplined methods a tax upon my Whitehall calm and patience; but here once again was Jack Adams, remorseless and violent in pursuit of his ideals. He soon found that it was unnecessary and time-wasting to

157

belabour us with histrionic tirades. There was a job to be done and to be done quickly. He became no less critical, but constructively so, and he deployed in argument and discussion qualities which I had come to associate with Churchill—relentless probing and questioning, an invincible refusal to accept negative and inactive responses, and a lionhearted resolve to get on with the job. Out of school he was friendly and humorous, never long at rest, darting from one occupation to another, a man of boundless energy, the wiry toughness of his approach to everything belying the loose figure tending to obesity, the happy moon face and the rather husky singer's voice.

Headmasters of Public Schools are not usually to be found in the rebel class. They must at any rate uphold their own authority and exercise effective control over their school. Occasionally they are rebels against the system or parts of the system and they introduce novel ideas of punishment, new methods of teaching, liberal notions of discipline and so on. In the twenties there was an inclination in some schools to introduce a system by which boys only learnt what they wanted to and in their own time. Nowadays fagging is abolished and the prefectorial system, the pride and wonder of the Arnold tradition, is under fire. But the headmasters whom I have discussed were not rebels in the definitions of this chapter. They were, by compulsion of their office, authoritarian. Henry Kendall, for all his restless exuberance and dynamic energy, was very suspicious of radical attitudes and seemed always anxious to believe that the Government, in all walks of life, could do no wrong. The only sign of rebelliousness he ever gave was a contempt for convention in manners and appearance. Nobody seeing him rolling round the fields in untidy clothes or grotesquely tattered hats or listening to the continuous mumbling of anecdote in his very individual style, would have guessed that he was an unswerving supporter of the Establishment—but he was. University dons are in a different position again. Most of them would not wish to rebel against the institution which gave them their livelihood, but they would not hesitate to feed into the minds of their pupils rebellious ideas of every kind. That is part of the meaning of university education, the free exchange of ideas. In our age no penalty is attached to the public denial of the existence of God and poor Shelley could have published his thesis without any fear of the consequences. Academic freedom, the freedom to teach what you like and in what terms, is the banner which university dons carry proudly into battle. Some of them would take this devotion to the cause of freedom to a point of rebellion against any authority or control; but these are not lovers of learning. They come near to being iconoclasts.

The influence of very clever young dons who succumb too readily to the temptation of stimulating adolescent minds, eager and unstable, is without doubt a contributory factor in the restless and dangerous disaffection of undergraduates. A love of cruelty and destruction is a part of original sin. A child will torment and wound insects and animals. Boys will bully weaker boys. Young men will wreck trains and kindle bonfires with other people's property. Unless this human inclination to wanton demolition is corrected by a parallel growth of social conscience, we are on the broken road to anarchy. When dons, taking advantage of this destructive bent in their disciples, translate their aspirations into the intellectual and spiritual world and teach them that all accepted codes, all institutions, all human achievements have no meaning and no value, then they are in coalition with other unseen powers whose unspoken aim is, not just rebellion, but the crude obliteration of all images, all idols, all heroes, all ideals.

The natural rebel is not an iconoclast. The iconoclast will pull down every image he can see, trample on all your cherished beliefs, sneer at your principles, despise and reject your simple notions of love and service, denounce every form of religion as superstition, and give you nothing in return. He is a destroyer, holding nothing sacred and nothing dear. A rebel is more positive and constructive. He is alienated and disgusted by the performance of authority, not because he wants to demolish every kind of authority, but because he can see quite clearly how much better authority might be exercised. He rebels against what he hates because he knows what he loves. If he loves nothing he is an iconoclast. The rebel is moved and stimulated by a divine discontent. Anyone who has no touch of that deserves to be called smug. He is a man who wants no change, content with what he has, anxious to keep it, longing for the world to stand still so that he can enjoy the place and position he has won for himself. He is the man who hid his talent in the ground. That may not be discreditable, but it is dull and the world were a dull place if the Pharisees were always in charge. The founder of the Christian religion was a rebel of rebels but he could hardly be called an iconoclast.

Chapter VII

OTHER VOWS AND VOCATIONS

When I passed my daily working life, both in the war and for many years thereafter, in the company of Ministers, senior civil servants, the great chiefs of the three Services, Ambassadors and so on, I became an object of envy amongst some of my acquaintances. 'What a lot of interesting people you must meet,' they would constantly say. My previous chapters will give an idea about the extent of the interest they had for me. Many of them were, of course, very interesting personalities and they were exercising these personalities in exciting and important circumstances; but I do not feel sure that most of them were any more interesting or important than the men one meets in less exalted situations. What is interesting about men is their ability to do their jobs and to do them well. Meetings of Rotary Clubs can be dull, pedestrian affairs, except when a man, who knows and loves his own job, is explaining it enthusiastically. I do not remember any public discourse which gave me more pleasure and enlightenment than a talk at a Rotary Club lunch in Whitehaven about the origins, the characteristics and the care of Herdwick Sheep. I was anxious, therefore, not to give any impression that I thought that the professions and occupations I have so far described were the only ones that carried power and importance. Consequently I have added in this chapter a few sketches of men of a quite different stamp, working in fields where I have seldom worked, and exercising a profound influence on other men.

The power of the Tycoon is very great. Industries, employing thousands of human beings, fail and prosper in accordance with his decisions. He appears to open and shut factories at will, dismissing workers in one place and taking on more in another. But of course his will is far from unhampered. He is nowadays far too ready to listen to charlatans who mesmerise him with the false jargon of management techniques and personnel administration. There are, too, all kinds of economic trends in world markets, which he cannot control and which often force him, willy-nilly, into decisions. What hampers him most, he would probably claim, is the economic and fiscal policy of the Government, the credit squeezes, the taxation, the devaluation of money and so on, by which the Chancellor of the Exchequer in a two-hour speech in the House of Commons can frustrate and perhaps destroy his careful plans for a five-year expansion and development. Whether he enjoys a power which can be so suddenly dislocated and suppressed is a matter for wonder. In my very narrow acquaintance with industry it has struck me that the Chairman of a Board of Directors is much more than *primus inter pares,* with far more direct authority over the Board than even the most autocratic of Prime Ministers dares to exert over his Cabinet. Perhaps some men enjoy this distinctive power but it carries with it terrible responsibilities. John Davies, then Minister of Technology, said that, although the desire to have authority over others is not inborn in every individual, for those who aspire persistently to increase their authority the joy in exercising it is real and the reward in doing so very satisfying. This could perhaps be said of any occupation and any profession. The popular theory that captains of industry are interested only in making large profits for themselves and their shareholders—but mostly for themselves—cannot be seriously sustained. Industries exist to make things which people in this country and overseas want and the aim of the good industrialist is to make these things better than anyone else either at home or abroad. To do this he must make profits to allow him to expand and improve. Without profits he will stagnate and perish. This makes good sense and is the secret of economic success in any country.

I wonder sometimes, however, whether in both commercial and industrial undertakings, the object of profit-making is not sometimes forgotten. Mergers and take-overs, groupings and regroupings, constantly take place but the products remain the same. Somebody perhaps gets more power but the worker and the customer seem to go on much as before. I have expressed the same doubt about the effect of the moves and counter-moves of party political life. When one considers the realm of King-makers and un-King-makers, perplexity increases; but you can still see the readers of the *Daily Mirror,* in the morning crush, intent upon the pabulum served up and quite unaware of the difference between the cowslip and the kingcup.

The power of writers of all kinds, editors, journalists, authors, biographers and poets, can be very great. Journalists and editors of daily and weekly journals would hope, I think, that their opinions, ingeniously expressed and carefully selected, had great influence upon the political and artistic attitudes of the day. In fact they do, less so in politics perhaps than in the arts. The daily newspapers, for the most part slanted in favour of the Conservative Party, seem to have less effect upon electoral results than one might expect, and in spite of editorial admonishments a good many of the readers of the *Daily Express* apparently vote Labour. If political commentators and leader writers wish to exercise power over the electorate and think that they do so, they must often be disappointed. On the other hand there is no doubt that they inform the public and most of them take pains to inform the public correctly. If that is not exactly power it is a service which must bring its own satisfaction.

In the world of plays and books and music, indeed in all the arts, the critics have great influence over their readers, far more than the authors and artists themselves find acceptable. The critic comes between the author and his public and the author fears that, if the critic says a book is worthless and unreadable, nobody will read it. This fear may be exaggerated and it is probably true that if there were no critics fewer books would be read, fewer plays attended and so on. Moreover, the critic must himself have considerable literary gifts and a compelling style before readers will take note of him. The trouble sometimes is that a critic earns a wide reputation by the liveliness of his perceptions and the pungency of his style and then, perhaps because it causes him less labour, falls into a strain of malevolence and 'cuts up', as Macaulay used to call it, every book that is put before him without reading it. Nevertheless in the history of English literature the critic holds an honourable place. Hazlitt, for example, writes with gusto, in a style rich and dynamic. He does not keep personal spite out of some of his judgments, but I should think that he has, over the past 150 years, brought a great many people to an admiration of Wordsworth, whom Hazlitt attacked and belaboured at times maliciously; but Hazlitt never lost sight of the fact,

163

nor let his readers do so, that he was writing, or lecturing, about a man whose genius out-topped most of his contemporaries.

Macaulay made his name as a critic and his clear-cut style and terse and pithy sentences have won him many devoted imitators ever since. He is brilliantly prejudiced, arrogant and self-assured; but the fact that he 'cut up', most unfairly, Croker's edition of Boswell's *Life of Johnson* has certainly added to the number of readers of that immortal work. The critic performs a useful service, which is often gracefully and attractively performed, but when he forgets that the limelight is supposed to shine upon the author and not upon himself he risks becoming vulgar, obtrusive and unfair.

In these days a new type of critic has come to the front—the television interviewer. The purpose of the television interview is to allow the subject of the interview to disclose his personality and his opinions. To achieve this requires from the interviewer a degree of self-effacing wisdom—a quality which only a few habitually exhibit. Too often the interviewer seems to feel it is his job to score points, to lay traps, to *win* the interview as if it were a contest—a very one-sided contest too because the interviewer makes the rules as he goes along and is his own referee. There is too much power in the hands of these men and they seem to relish it too much.

Many authors write with the simple intention of giving pleasure to others, and it is certainly true that if this is not any part of their intention their books are likely to be very dull and not very influential. Novelists are not moralists. They are narrators, observers, psychologists. They set their characters in a background, graphically delineated, and watch their mutual reactions with intense and subtle perception. There may be a moral in the tale, but it is not their first aim to drive it home. Dickens, the most sensitive and observant of them all, never sacrificed his endlessly inventive imagination to a virtuous determination to be a reforming philanthropist. Thackeray's moralising is tedious but superficial, and George Eliot never attempted it. They have power, these novelists, not a definable power for which they aimed, but an undefinable and unsought power, the power to extend the thought and imagination of men and to enlarge their human understanding and compassion. Theirs is a power very different from the politician's or from the schoolmaster's but no less, perhaps more, significant. In my own life, amongst the many influences which affect the daily workings of my mind and the exercise of my personality, I should estimate as very great the influence of the author of *David Copperfield*.

When it comes to poets we enter a different world, a much less calculating world, a world in which impulses and enthusiasms play a compelling part, and genius takes its own unpredictable way. It would be difficult to say that poets, except perhaps didactic poets (if that is not a contradiction in terms) had any motive to exert power and influence over others, except only as a man might, in an excess of good humour and fellowship, strive to embrace neighbours, acquaintances and friends in his own warm concepts of the significance of life and human nature. It is hardly possible to imagine Shakespeare scheming and designing to exert power over others. He was an actor and a playwright, dedicated to giving pleasure to audiences of all types and classes. But he had this power and influence and he would be astonished to find that 350 years later men were dissecting and evaluating his influence, his philosophy, his intentions. His power over the men and women of this generation is immeasurable, but this object was never in his mind. He was a journeyman, but a journeyman inspired in a way which no one can explain or understand. Wordsworth might be thought to have been a more deliberate power-seeker, more anxious to exert his influence over the taste and feelings of other men. But in his early and greatest period this was not the case. He was 'a man speaking to men', not preaching to them; and his object was to mark for them in the language of the human heart their relationship with the natural world and in his own words, 'to bind together by passion and knowledge the vast empire of human society'—an ambitious aim certainly, but not a bid for personal power over others. Later in life, having satisfied himself by the composition of *The Prelude* that he had the necessary powers he wrote *The Excursion*; and *The Excursion,* elaborately didactic, is the failure of self-assurance. *The Prelude,* a work of warm and natural humility, convinced him that he was gifted with some superior power and it was precisely at that moment that this superior power deserted him. The power of true poets over the hearts of men is the power of religion, to elevate, to stimulate, to move to humility and compassion. They do not seek this power but in the exercise of their true function, 'to transmute almost any experience into poetry' and 'to apply imagination to every aspect of life', as Dr Gittings says of Keats, they abundantly achieve it.

In the same category as poets come composers and artists and all men of original genius, who, as it were, set out to do a simple thing, and, by the mere exercise of their inner powers, create a masterpiece. It is a simple thing, simple in the sense of straightforward and uncomplicated, not easy, to set out to paint a landscape. Thousands do it every day and in the summer months the easels and sketch books of amateurs are a permanent feature of the countryside; but only a Constable or a Cotman can add 'the light that never was on sea or land'. The likeness of a particular man becomes under the hand of Rembrandt the image of mankind with all the depth of human suffering in the eyes, the lines of anxious perplexity about the face, and round the mouth a convulsive touch, perhaps, of joy and laughter. Rembrandt painted that man to please him, to please his family, and to earn some money. He had no idea in his head, no ambition, to exert a mysterious power over the thoughts and feelings of succeeding generations.

The composer works in a medium which to the majority of men is incomprehensible. They cannot even think of a simple tune and if they could they would have no idea how to write it down or play it. The composer, using a language of which only the alphabet can be learned by rote, expresses his ideas, concepts, feelings, emotions in sounds; and these sounds convey even to the listener, if he surrenders to their magic, thoughts and emotions far beyond the traffic of his every day. They need not be, and almost certainly are not, the thoughts and emotions which inspired the composer to express himself in sound. That is a mystery, and the mystery is deeper still when one remembers that before the age of 40 Beethoven was stone deaf and never himself heard the abundant richness and power of the sounds with which he has elevated, delighted and fortified his myriads of listeners and admirers. This power, this compelling power, over the feelings of others during the last 180 years was not desired or expected by Beethoven. He did as his violent genius told him.

These men of original genius, the writers and artists and composers, had no deliberate intention to exercise power over others, but, by following the mysterious beckonings of their nature and dedicating themselves to their inevitable calling, they have influenced and inspired sensitive human beings, unknown to them in their own generation and in succeeding generations unthought of and unimagined. Men of the world, men of action, are happy to acknowledge their debt. General Wolfe found Gray's *Elegy* a work of human genius far out-stripping the military art. John Stuart Mill and Edward Grey, very different characters but both deeply involved in the political activities of their times, found support and consolation in the poetry of Wordsworth. In our own time Wavell spent his scanty leisure from the crushing demands of war in the Middle East in making a selection of the poetry he liked best and knew by heart. Attlee, it seems, was deeply moved by the poetry of Vita Sackville West and in a critical hour in the history of our survival Churchill found inspiration in a poem by Arthur Hugh Clough. Examples can be multiplied. No power is greater or deeper than the power, unsought and unexpected, of these men of original genius.

That priests, of any kind of religion, have power is undeniable. But its exercise is more obvious in authoritarian types of church. In times past in this country when the rate of illiteracy was very high, the Roman Catholic priest wielded enormous authority and, in Chaucer's opinion, in a fashion greedy and unscrupulous. In the reformed Church of England in this age the priest cannot exact unquestioning obedience from a captive flock; and indeed this would not be, in the opinion of most Anglican clergymen, the function of the priest-hood. In the Church of England there are many mansions, but on the whole there is more breadth than height about it. All are welcome and many shades of opinion and belief can be fitted in. The Anglican priest is very rarely a dogmatic preacher, a cold and inaccessible law giver. He is much more like a social welfare worker, and with the decline of church-going in this country his services, the prayer and praise which he offers to God on behalf of his congregation, are very sparsely attended. This part of his ministration, the provision of a link between the laity and their God, is in constant demand only when people in his parish want to be baptised, married and buried; he then becomes the broker of hatch, match and despatch. The motives of men seeking ordination are quite unknown to me, but I cannot believe that one of them is the desire to exercise power over others. Many priests, however, do in fact exert great influence by the saintliness of their living, like Chaucer's parish priest :—

But Christes lore, and his apostles twelve,
He taughte, and at first he folwed it himselve.

Another power, stimulating but more ephemeral, is the power of the eloquent preacher. I should find it difficult, if not impossible, to recall the content of any sermon I ever listened to; but I can remember occasions when I felt uplifted and came away from the church, serious and determined to lead a more Christian life. The earliest of these was my Confirmation in St Luke's, Chelsea by the then Bishop of London, Dr Winnington Ingram. I daresay his sermon was in no way remarkable and had often been preached before, but the figure of the Bishop in the pulpit and the rather unusual tones of his voice have remained in my memory. I was very young and very impressionable and that elevated man of God helped my wandering and immature thoughts on that important day.

I happened to be staying in Folkestone one Eastertide just before I went up to Oxford and my mother and I went into Holy Trinity Church on Good Friday intending to stay for half, or less, of the three-hour service—a practice quite common in those days. The compelling eloquence of the vicar, The Revd. W. H. Elliott, held us, unreluctant captives, for the full stretch of those devotions. Later on, Elliott filled St Michael's, Chester Square, for many years and was a popular publicist for the Christian religion. If on reflection the effect of eloquent sermons seems to be transitory—and this is often said of Billy Graham —there is no doubt that sermons to which one listens with excited attention become a permanent part of one's consciousness of Christianity. It is the same in the secular world. Few things are less rewarding than reading the speeches of statesmen long since dead. Out of the contemporary context, the turmoil of current events, without the tones of voice or the emphasising gestures, they seem flat and dull; and I imagine that even now young men, reading those clarion speeches of Churchill which gave us the courage to survive in 1940, will wonder why.

Nevertheless the power of the orator is, in his own lifetime, sudden and formidable. Without the violent exercise of that particular power, the world might have been spared the tragic sufferings of the Second World War. It is no doubt true that political and social circumstances in Germany and Italy between the wars made them ripe for revolutionary change. But the false and inhuman creeds of Nazism and Fascism would have made no triumphant headway without the manic oratory of Hitler and Mussolini, both of whom knew how to rouse the passions of the mob. Some merciful quality in our own national character—a sense of humour, a love of moderation—protected us from the strutting pretensions of Oswald Mosley.

All professional men exercise power of some kind even if they stay within the comparatively narrow confines of their profession. Technologists, by their professional powers, make practical new ways of life—new roads and bridges to suit man's increasing passion for movement and speed, new houses and flats designed at one and the same time to provide man with a degree of ease and comfort and hygiene which earlier generations never imagined and to make the most economical use of the overburdened earth. If technologists are sometimes thought to be practical and unimaginative, uninterested in the spiritual unspoken longings of man, the landings on the moon must have given the lie to that idea. It was the technologists who opened the door and let in upon an astonished human race real pictures of the Earth taken by men standing on the moon looking across the moon's horizon. Without their professional skill men could never have done this and returned safely to Earth. They deserve even more honour and renown than the technologists of the age of Prince Albert, some of whom are, rather surprisingly, commemorated by stained-glass windows in the north aisle of the nave of Westminster Abbey!

Honour and renown are what professional men do for the most part seek—to be the best, the most skilled, the most punctilious, the most imaginative, engineer, lawyer, doctor, architect and so on. They do not seek power, they seek fame and admiration and a feeling of inner satisfaction that they have achieved the highest standards of their calling and perhaps advanced its frontiers. Some men, notably lawyers and accoun-

169

tants, sometimes step outside the confines of their own profession to seek wider responsibilities and more direct power in politics and industry. But for the most part the lawyer will set his sights at the top of his profession and advance by progressive experience and skill to a judgeship or a leading solicitor's practice in the City of London or elsewhere. He is not looking for power but for wider fields of responsibility in which to perform his professional services, so carefully cultivated and improved. Many men are attracted into the medical profession by profound feelings of mercy and compassion, with no ambition in their heads but to help and console the sick and the suffering. That is the supreme art of the general practitioner as it is of the parish priest. The enormous extension of medical knowledge and its fragmentation into a great number of specialisms has transmuted the art of medicine to the science of medicine; but in the whole profession, famous surgeons, notable consultants, medical research scientists, general practitioners, there is no thought of power, no desire to dominate. The ruling ambition is still to heal and console, to conquer the bodily and mental afflictions of humanity, and to probe deeper and deeper into the mystery of human life.

Professional men comprise a most attractive class. They have no desire to dominate and direct other people. Their only ambition is to excel in their own profession, and, if perhaps from time to time they are envious of others, it is not usually a personal envy, not a venomous hostility against an individual, but simply a burning desire to improve their professional skill, to master their techniques, and to appear more masterful, more skilful and more successful than anyone else in their profession. I do not think that the truly great professionals, in any sphere of human activity think in terms of personal rivalry and competition. They want to be supreme, not in order to demolish and diminish others, but because they hope that their efforts will establish higher standards in their particular sphere. They have about them a most encouraging self-confidence, without any touch of vanity or conceit. They know that they know. They are not proud about it or ostentatious. They do not boast and they make no pretences. They are modest men because, although they have an easy assurance about them, they are inwardly tormented by the Socratic wisdom of knowing how much they do not know.

In the world of sport the highest type of professional is never satisfied with his performance. He can always do better, he continually tells himself; and, as soon as that constant voice ceases to repeat its charge, he declines and deteriorates. He has another delightful characteristic; he never sneers at the struggling amateur. He is happy to play the game with him, to help and encourage him without any sort of patronising admonishment, and above all to enjoy the association however unequal. It is a pleasure, rare and refreshing, to consort with such men or to see and listen to them. In cricket the destination of the Ashes is to me less significant, less absorbing, than the professional concentration of, for example, John Edrich or Ray Illingworth. The quality and value of antiques are less interesting to me than the professional assurance and the real modesty of Arthur Negus in handling them.

There are, of course, professional men who are not content with the narrow ascending steps of their own profession, who do not see a gay and beckoning light at the top of the stairway. I have already mentioned lawyers and accountants, and in other chapters I have talked more fully about public servants, fighting men, schoolmasters and dons. I cannot think of a professional cricketer who deviated into a political career, though I can certainly think of some outstanding athletes who did so. It is not a rule without exception, but a generally accepted fact, that professional men like their professions and resist all blandishments to leave them. Even the Headship of an Oxford or Cambridge College, once considered a comfortable prize, giving its occupant dignity and influence and importance, will with great difficulty entice the professional from his skills. The true professional is a dedicated man not to be diverted from the pursuit of a single excellence. When Antisthenes was told that a certain Ismenias played excellently upon the flute, he replied, 'Then he is good for nothing else; otherwise he would not have played so well'. That is not a sneer; it is a tribute to professionalism.

Chapter VIII

THE POWER OF WOMEN

It is obvious, the reader may say, that I have been talking about two kinds of power, the power which a particular office confers, and the power of human personality. Others may protest that I should more precisely define my terms; sometimes I am talking about power, sometimes about influence. On the latter objection a long, difficult and rather dull book could be written. For myself I doubt very much if there can be influence without power or any significant power without influence. As for the first objection, if it is an objection, it is perfectly true that the office of Prime Minister confers much wider power upon its occupant than the office of headmaster. But the office itself has no power, whether it be the Cabinet room or the headmaster's study. The power is in the hands of the occupant; the personality is what counts. The headmaster, who sits smugly in his study, drawing up liberal timetables and elaborate precepts of organisation, has very little power if the assistant masters and the boys pay no attention and go on much as before. As for the Prime Minister, 'Pitt was to Addington as London was to Paddington'; and it is certain that in the last years of his Prime Ministership Ramsay MacDonald had very little power or influence of any kind. The personality, once so magnetic and even magnificent, degenerated into empty vanities and meaningless verbiage; and with this personal degeneration the power of the office went into commission. The same might be said of Churchill himself in the last years of his last Premiership, and the attempt by Eden to make the office of Prime Minister more powerful and decisive than it ought to be led to his own tragedy. Oliver Cromwell was succeeded by his hapless son, Tumbledown Dick. Certainly office confers power at every level, but only the right personality will use it effectively. There are many jacks-in-office in modern society, far too many men of mean spirit and unusual ignorance, who use their office—whether it be the conductorship of a 'bus or a clerkship in the Post Office—as a strong shield behind which they can safely exert that puny officiousness to which their nature inclines them. But in the deep significance of life this ridiculous pomposity produces in others not much more than temporary and superficial irritation. The men discussed in this book are well above this ignoble level and all of them, I believe, have tried to use the powers of their office for the common good. They have tried, and their failure or success is in large part a result of their own personalities. What, then, makes personality? I have already referred to heredity, environment, the personalities and attitudes of parents, the influence of active schoolmasters and learned dons. These all play their part in the creation of a personality. I have said nothing directly so far about the influence of women and, because their influence upon men is so profound, I devote my last chapter to them.

Some of my early recollections are of the suffragettes and of the turmoil and destruction which their violent demonstrations gave rise to. They had a strong inclination to martyrdom in the cause—chaining themselves to railings, starving themselves in prison, even a suicide under the hooves of the King's horse in the Derby, insulting the Prime Minister, planting bombs, and generally organising violence, threats and disorder in public places, and giving London policemen an accurate foretaste of the angry hostility which their successors were to face in Grosvenor Square fifty years later. These women wanted the vote, because they wanted at least that tiny say in the government of their country, and in any case they refused to accept that their menfolk were any better qualified to exercise the vote than they were. The First World War put a stop to their revolutionary agitations and women became involved in rendering service of many kinds to their country. They made munitions, they nursed the wounded, they joined the fighting Services, they worked on the land and so on. It was this variety of service and their devotion to arduous duty, far more than the tumult and commotion of the Suffragette movement, which finally earned them the vote and brought to Westminster the first women M.P.s. In political terms this brought them into equality with men and in consequence it gave them a power which they did not have before, without taking away from them the power which belongs peculiarly to their sex. Now, fifty years later, Mrs Pankhurst stands serene upon her pedestal

173

close to the Palace of Westminster, towards which she had exhibited such venomous hostility, her mission accomplished, and all passion spent. Since her day there have been a number of women M.P.s and some women Cabinet Ministers. In the performance of these duties they have demonstrated that women can do what used to be called men's work, but those who have been outstandingly successful have owed their success to the masculine qualities of their intellect and the courage and tenacity of their characters, and not to those essentially feminine characteristics which have given women so much power down the ages. They have not necessarily lacked these characteristics, but they are not the characteristics which they have needed to put to use in the political world. The same could be said of those women civil servants who have reached the top of their professions. They are tough, they are powerful in argument and negotiation; they need to be. Some of them, I have no doubt, cast away this formidable armour in their private lives and turn their hearts in gentleness and kindness to their families. If Florence Nightingale had compassion for the sick and suffering, she had little for Sidney Herbert, whom she hounded and badgered remorselessly. Few men would have driven so hard.

Women have always shone in any profession that has been opened to them, on the stage of course, in medicine ônce Elizabeth Garrett Anderson had cleared the way, in scholarship and in letters, more especially in the novel. Why should this not be so? Some women are irritated by expressions of surprise and wonder at their accomplishments. Dr Johnson was by no means contemptuous about Fanny Burney's incursion into literature with *Cecilia* and *Evelina*. She was soon surpassed by Miss Austen, and among the great novelists of the Victorian age few stars shone more brightly than the Brontës and George Eliot. But these great novelists—except perhaps in some peculiarities of observation here and there—might as well have been men; and they would have scorned the appellation 'authoress', as if there were some difference or distinction between the original productions of the male and female mind. 'Actress' is acceptable because the femininity is to be seen; but 'poetess' has an air of patronage about it which was very much resented by Alice Meynell. I am sure Mrs Castle would not have cared to have been addressed as 'Ministress'. Such notable women have their own fame, and their influence upon others is of the same kind as the influence of men in the same professions. The power exercised by Mrs Castle must be compared with the power exercised by any Minister of the Crown. George Eliot and the Brontës invite comparison with Dickens and Thackeray, Elizabeth Barrett Browning may be considered with her husband, not so much as his wife, but as an equal poet.

Most married women, however, whether they have artistic and intellectual ability or not, would regard their lives as dedicated to husbands and children. I have known women who have added to this dedication professional accomplishments of their own—eminence in scientific research, the mastery of administrative techniques, the control of a university institution —without in any way detracting from the normal service of a woman to her family. It is rare, perhaps, and no man could attempt it. There are some women who pursue with their husbands the same career, whose names are thus linked together—Sidney and Beatrice Webb, for example, who, after spending their honeymoon in inspecting trade societies in Ireland and attending the Trades Union Congress in Glasgow, dedicated their life partnership—'The firm of Webb' as she called it—to the advocacy of Socialism in various forms. But that is an unusual kind of marriage. Usually a woman's influence, unexpressed and unavowed, is with the members of her own family. How can I help my husband to succeed, to win place and position, fame and honour? How can I help my children to grow up strong and resolute to confront and conquer the dangers and disappointments of life? And there are questions even deeper than those, which tear and torment her inmost heart in waking anxious hours. There are, it is true, many women—as there are men—vain and flippant, who never ask themselves such pompous tiresome questions and whose sole interest is worldly success and enough money to mix in a trivial society, flaunting the fashions of the day. There are others whose attitudes are supine, reactions negative, content to be spoiled themselves and to spoil and suckle their children. But I am writing of women of courage and character who live their lives for others, for husband and children, some more for the one than for the other. Their influence is very great, but not always beneficial.

It would be difficult, perhaps, to prove convincingly that

the influence exercised by Cleopatra over Julius Caesar and Antony was of particular advantage to them or to Egypt or to the Roman Empire. It would be impossible to deny that both these very considerable men—Julius, indeed, much more than that—fell under her sway. Plutarch tells us that there was great variety in her powers of conversation. 'Her physical beauty was neither astonishing nor inimitable; but it derived a force from her wit, and her fascinating manner, which was absolutely irresistible. Her voice was delightfully melodious and the same variety of modulation as an instrument of many strings.' Against such a combination of charms Antony had no power to put up any resistance. Indeed charms of far less intensity often achieve a domination of masculine will power. When I was in the Army in the Second World War, I was at first much alarmed and much deflated by the stock security story, drummed into the ears of novices, that some Colonel in the careless ecstasy of copulation had revealed to his mistress the D-Day of some vital operation. The information was misused. As Baldwin said about the Press Lords of his time they enjoyed what had been the prerogative of the harlot down the ages—power without responsibility. Mistresses have great influence over men and they use it in many different ways. Where the relationship between a man and his mistress is skin deep, and little more, the woman, maybe, will use her carnal power for selfish ends, demanding clothes, jewels, money by the threat of favours refused or by the unscrupulous use of blackmail. But the relationship often goes much deeper than that, especially when a man's married life is unhappy and unrewarding, but for one reason or another indissoluble. Then the mistress assumes more of the wife's role, and influences and counsels her lover over the pursuit of his career—or the career which for some reasons of her own she is determined he shall follow. Aspasia, it is traditionally believed, not only gave delight to Pericles in his leisure hours, but was his strength and stay in the arduous and dangerous progress of an Athenian statesman. According to Plutarch when he was separated from his wife 'he took Aspasia for whom he had the tenderest regard; insomuch that he never went out upon business, or returned without saluting her'. And it is alleged that intelligent Athenians, including Socrates, believed that she was the author of the famous funeral oration. An

American woman, twice divorced, in a surprised terror at the extent of her power, caused the abdication of a King and sent a tremor through the ancient foundations of the British Empire.

A husband who has chosen wisely never tires of acknowledging his debt to his wife not only for her constant support in the progress of his career but for deeper and often incommunicable reasons. Mrs Gladstone, in her own right beautiful, attractive, gay and delightful, was completely wrapped up in her husband's career. This took overriding priority in her life, even though her impulsive nature made her at times forgetful and unpunctual in the performance of the duties of a political hostess. In return Gladstone adored her and confided in her all his secrets, while deep in his granite heart this stern and covenanting man was mellowed and softened into a gentler humility by her grace and her devotion. The high places of this world can be isolated and cold for a lonely occupant. In this century two kings have been sustained by the watchful affection and devotion, unceasing and unswerving, of their consorts; while a third rejected the remote eminence of kingship because he was denied that support. It is hard to define this sustaining power which in most circumstances a wife alone can exercise. It does not always come from her active participation and interest in her husband's job. Too much zeal in that direction can be counter-productive, irritation at female domination, and accusations from without of petticoat government. It is very easy to detect which partner wears the trousers and to see through the pitiful pretence of 'My husband always says . . . ' and 'It was my husband's wish entirely' and so on.

There are many examples, confronting us daily, of married couples who live in great contentment, each in almost total ignorance of what the other really does. The man wonders where the money goes to, why there is so much fuss and trouble, why it is so difficult to get a simple meal, why it takes so long to pack, why he must always be kept waiting—and endless more trivialities which, without bothering to understand, he finds irritating; but the irritation in the end becomes a part of his love and occupies an odd little corner of his heart.

The woman would be hard put to it to explain to a stranger what her husband does. She could name his profession but if pressed to expand and expound his daily work she would soon be embarrassed and confounded. And yet they would not live without each other, without the warm intimacies of married life, without the sharing of joy and sorrow, without the desolation of parting and the deep happiness of reuniting, without the speechless signs of understanding and encouragement. The man, perhaps, needs this more than the woman; the widower is almost always more lost and more wretched than the widow. There are many marriages in which intimacy is dead and companionship forgotten. They have been replaced by indifference, the comings and goings unnoticed, the joys and sorrows unshared. In these circumstances the woman has no power. In one marriage I knew about, the partnership remained undissolved because love had given place to hatred, and the wife had persevered in the daily routine of dispute and discomfort with the sole object of tormenting and destroying her husband. That is a satanic power, rare and detestable.

The power of a mother over her sons is different in origin and different in kind. When the mother is the kind of woman who enjoys domination, she has rare opportunities for its exercise. Children cannot escape the daily discipline of love and care imposed by their mothers and it is usually the case that sons are more responsive to it than daughters. Mothers are severely criticised and vilified if they are believed to desire and devise the complete domination and possession of their sons and to resist to the uttermost the cutting of the silver cord. It is very seldom, I think, that a mother desires nothing else but possession of her sons. It is not so rare for her to desire to act through her sons, to express through them her own strength of character, to achieve in their name the ambitions which her sex denied her. For example Coriolanus, according to Plutarch 'pursued glory because the acquisition of it delighted Volumnia, his mother. For when she was witness to the applause he received, when she saw him crowned, when she embraced him with tears of joy, then it was that he reckoned himself at the height of honour and felicity. He thought he could never sufficiently express his tenderness and respect. He even married in compliance with her desire and request, and after his wife had borne him children, still lived in the same house with his mother'.

When George III was a young prince his mother's influence

was paramount. She protected him from any wider or more liberal contacts with society, she prevented the first marriage proposed for him and set her face firmly against suggestions that he should leave her tutelage and establish his own household. She herself had been brought up in a petty German court and had stored up in her mind ideas about its proper conduct. Her son must behave autocratically and independently —as she would have behaved if she had been a regnant Grand Duchess—and all her admonishments to her son, *To be King,* were derived from her own narrow origins and experience. She could not see the difference between Saxe Gotha and the United Kingdom.

Oliver Cromwell was devoted to his mother and owed much to her. She sympathised deeply with the high aims of his tortured career—perhaps did something to inspire them—but she mistrusted the worldly trappings and grandeur which surrounded the Lord Protector. She had no such ambitions for her son; and just before she died, at the age of 93, she expressed her true feeling for him in this blessing which she gave him :

The Lord cause His face to shine
upon you, and comfort you in all
your adversities, and enable you to
do great things for the glory of the
most High God, and to be a relief unto
His people. My dear son, I leave
my heart with thee : Good night.

It is natural that mothers should desire success for their sons, the kind of success, sometimes perhaps, which their husbands failed to achieve; and beyond success, strength of character and happiness of mind, compassionate feelings and an interest in those things, books, music, beauty of art and nature, which have brought them abiding joy. Their influence is very great in these directions, instinctive, perhaps, more than deliberate, exercised more by example than by precept. I picked up a book not long since in a friend's house, a book about poetry, and written in the fly leaf was a short inscription by the author :

To my beloved mother without whose love nothing
good or beautiful would ever have been known to me.

If that seems a trifle sentimental. it expresses, nevertheless, in a few words what most sensitive men feel about their mothers.

Arnold Toynbee is more precise and more particular about his acknowledgments, and when he comes to the end of his monumental Study of History he thanks his mother for making him an historian : 'My mother awakened in me a lifelong interest in history by communicating to me her own interest in it at a very early stage of my life . . . if my mother had not given my mind—and heart too—this early bent, I am sure that I should not ever have written this book; so she bears some responsibility for the undertaking'. And a little further on in the list of acknowledgments he is more particular : 'My mother introduced me to Robert Browning . . . in the Christmas holidays of A.D. 1905-6, my mother and I read Browning together. I can remember the evening, in the lamplight, when she opened a volume and said "I will begin with *My Star*; I wonder what you will think of it". Her pleasure at the prospect of sharing her love of Browning's poetry with me had opened my heart to the poet before I had heard a line'.

This is the kind of power which a fastidious and sensitive woman wishes to exercise over her sons, a gentle influence, but positive and strong, smoothing the roughness of life, mellowing its raw ugliness, softening its harsh masculinity, sustaining her sons in adversity and protecting them from surrender to the onslaughts of ruthless ambition in a rude materialist world.

The poet Wordsworth has not escaped the charge of enslaving his womenfolk, of using them as amanuenses, of imposing on them duties and functions which are usually the responsibility of the man. The imputations are to some extent true, but those who so easily make them have little idea of the stresses and strains to which men of genius are subject, their elemental strength in one direction and their strange weakness in another. In the day-to-day business of a family Wordsworth was inefficient. He was too easily fussed and upset and in consequence he not seldom mismanaged his mundane responsibilities. His eyes were frequently painfully strained, and penmanship, as he called it, caused him physical affliction and generally resulted in a confusing illegibility. His women—his wife, his sister and his sister-in-law—came to his rescue, and, realising the exceptional profundity of his feelings and the severity of his meditations, took these tasks upon themselves.

Even in his own day he was criticised for his pose of infallibility and the readiness of his family—his 'fireside divan', Keats called it—to accept the pose; and Keats is reported to have been rebuked by Mrs Wordsworth for arguing with her husband, 'Mr Wordsworth is never interrupted'. But there is, of course, another side to this; and Charles Lamb, who knew Wordsworth far more intimately than Keats knew him, gets the balance right. Writing to Wordsworth on 9 April, 1816, he has this to say about Wordsworth's terrible handwriting —manual-graphy as he calls it:

> I should not wonder if the constant making out of such paragraphs [in Wordsworth's hand] is the cause of that weakness in Mrs Wordsworth's eyes, as she is tenderly pleased to express it. Dorothy, I hear, has mounted spectacles; so you have deoculated two of your dearest relations in life. Well, God bless you, and continue to give you power to write with a finger of power upon our hearts what you fail to impress, in corresponding lucidness, upon our outward eyesight.

Wordsworth was lucky. His wife and his sister, and his sister-in-law also, recognised his genius, and willingly gave him their service. But in doing so they gave him something else. He was by temperament excessively masculine, there was sometimes a certain coldness in his personal relationships outside his family, an occasional hardness of feeling, 'a matter-of-factness' Coleridge called it, an undue touchiness in the face of criticism, and a deep, almost desperate, pessimism. He could have been a political publicist of high quality or a severe and scathing critic; his satirical talent was strong. But he became a poet, tender and devoted, and he was proud to acknowledge the influence upon him of his wife, and, more especially, his exquisite sister.

His wife's influence was pervasive and changeless. It sweetened every day and the humdrum irritations of married life dissolved and disappeared under its mellow radiance. It conquered the rough and ungovernable passions by its example of a 'wise passiveness'. The influence of Wordsworth's sister was more positive and more constructive, yet instinctive still, not deliberate and devised:

181

She gave me eyes, she gave me ears;
And humble cares and delicate fears;
A heart, the fountain of sweet tears;
And love and thought and joy.

This softening and mellowing process is by no means the
limit of woman's influence upon man. The tenderness of a
woman, her touch and her sympathy are rare in every sense
—unmatched in nature and not so often extended. Women
are commonly braver and tougher than men, their physical
strength more feeble but their spirit higher and their endurance
greater. The pain and the labour are theirs, and the courage
to triumph over them. When Euripides makes a woman declare
that she would rather stand in the forefront of the battle three
times than bear a child once, he is expressing what most
sensitive men feel about the other sex, misnamed the weaker.
Men admire this stoic fortitude and often find themselves
expected to emulate it. Women have little patience with men's
moans over a little pain or their malingering fancies. I
remember when I was a schoolmaster a boy in my House
went in a fit of idle melancholy to the Matron declaring, 'I
feel very run down, Matron', and all he got for his comfort
was the straight rejoinder, 'Well! you'd better run up again'.
Women have an instinct about this, usually right, and their
tender sympathy is not forthcoming unless it is deserved.

They are equally quick to detect vanity in their menfolk,
manifestations of self-esteem, assumptions of superiority
unjustified by fact; and their debunking methods are sometimes
all the more effective because they are an odd mixture of
admiration and reproof, a kiss on one cheek and a slap across
the other. When I was a very young man I once appeared
adorned for the first time in accord with the fashion of the
day in a richly coloured bow tie. My mother cast upon me a
penetrating ray of critical observation and after a long and
embarrassing silence of regard made her considered pronounce-
ment : 'Yes, I think it suits your particular form of ugliness'.
To my wife many years later I once recounted that at a period
of my life, during which I had been much tormented and
enraged by the incompetence and ill-temper of my superiors,
I had assuaged my rebellious impatience by inventing what I
called an apophthegm : 'Never descend to the level of those

above you'. 'Very clever,' she said, 'very witty; but why does it have to be that silly word?' These anecdotes are far from trivialities; if they were trivialities they would not be remembered. They are part of a much larger effect.

Women in some curious way are the natural and perennial guardians of certain standards and principles which guide the behaviour of men. This function of theirs, though elevated, is strictly circumscribed. The standards and principles are concerned with matters of taste and decency, decorum and seemliness. They have no connexion with abstract truth or public morality—matters about which most women are strangely indifferent and negligent. It is undeniably true that sensitive men with respect for their womenfolk will watch their manners, will not swear and belch, will mind their appearance, shave carefully, wash their hands, brush their hair, will not sprawl in unbuttoned disarray, will not puff out tobacco smoke in profuse clouds. It is not very many years ago that my mother positively forbade her brother to smoke a cigar in the drawing-room; and he, already nearly 70 years old, was ashamed to have asked and remembered, no doubt, the strict conventions of decency in which they had both been nurtured. Indeed many of these rules of behaviour are traditional, handed down, by example and precept, from generation to generation, until they have become instinctive, innate, ingrained. They have nothing to do with class or education. Good women exercise this particular influence, whatever their origin and in every kind of society. In one family I know errors of taste, lapses in decency of speech and behaviour are stigmatised by the materfamilias as 'dirty and rude'; and everyone in the family knows exactly what is meant.

This kind of influence goes wider still. Many women, however attractive and amusing and intelligent nature may have made them, are never quite content with what nature has done. As Shakespeare has it, 'God hath given you one face, and you make yourselves another'. This delight in artifice, this striving to improve on the Creator's model, extends far beyond the shallow business of make-up. Few women, in recounting a story, will stick to the truth and let the truth win its own reward of interest, surprise and laughter. No, they must embellish and invent, and twist the whole thing, if they possibly

183

can, into a triumph for themselves. If sometimes this handling seems contrived and even ungenerous it is venial. Most men, on the other hand, are careful to avoid exaggerations and immodest attitudes and to spoil their stories with colourless understatement. But if they should, in their cups perhaps, boast and blather, that well-known look of wifely contempt will soon unnerve and silence them. Women are much better critics of their men than they are of themselves. Men are lucky. This critical regard of women, their constant watchfulness, the anxious look, the shadow on the face, the turning aside, the withdrawn air—these are the warning signs. Men observing them will stop short, on the brink of the dreadful humiliation which follows a wilful fall from grace and a vulgar sacrifice of the high standards of conduct imposed on them by women. And in private should I rant and roar, and curse my fate, accusing in ill-considered terms the villainous folly of my enemies, I am gently enjoined—in the day-time 'It is no good saying about it', and at night 'Just lie quietly'.

Epilogue

When Voltaire makes Candide say : 'Cela est bien dit, mais il faut cultiver notre jardin'—he is not thinking or speaking about retirement. The phrase, like many another, has been taken from its context, altered and used by men about to retire as the stock answer to the inevitable question, 'What will you do with yourself now?' It is the stock answer and it may even be the sincere intention of most men as they close the office door for the last time. They will have no more of it, no more of the competition, the quest for power, the jealous protection of their own rights; they will shake off the official dust from their feet; they have no more interest, no engagement; it is all over now; thank God for it, and now they can cultivate their garden. It very rarely happens like that, and where it does death often comes early. It is not easy for a man to feel content with being set aside and ignored. Is experience worth nothing? Does nobody want to know that in the performance of his office he encountered all these snags and difficulties and valiantly fought his way through them? There is nothing new under the sun and if only they would ask him he could save them so much trouble. But they will not ask him, and that is just as well because there was never any wisdom or any profit to be obtained from leaning upon one's predecessor. Well! if there is no decent way in which he can keep one foot in his old camp, are there not many related activities where his experience would be valued? It is not good enough to stay at home brooding in idleness upon the stores of his experience so painstakingly acquired. Besides, retirement to his country home, so long wished for, premeditated with such delight, is not quite what he had hoped. There is no longer the habitual company of like-minded men, the daily discussions, the easy exchange of ideas. Neighbours do not drop in and if they do the conversation inclines towards Mr. Justice Shallow's, and reminiscences of the striking achievements of the dead are interrupted by enquiries about the price of bullocks and ewes.

Moreover the flow of domestic harmony is disturbed. Spheres of influence, long since established and regarded, have become blurred and ill-defined. The dominating attitudes of the office are out of place in the home and the rushed and excitable morning mood of the châtelaine differs strangely from the radiant evening welcome to which he has been for so long habituated.

Prime Ministers, as we have already noted, find it very difficult to retire and Ramsay Macdonald and Neville Chamberlain are to be envied for the timing of their departure, before a protracted old age subjected them to the meaningless anti-climax which tormented Winston and his family. Macmillan has sought refuge and relief in writing his memoirs and, if these occasionally bring down upon his head some reproofs for inaccuracy or unfair judgments, they are for the most part so full of wit and wisdom and so distinguished in style that politicians would be well advised to study them. Public servants are no less reluctant to retire than other men. Many of them find their way on to Boards of Directors, they sit on Royal Commissions and public Committees of Enquiry, they go into Local Government, they serve on Governing Bodies of schools and so on. Some, but very few, are bold enough to write books, but this is contrary to their traditions of silence and anonymity. It is a pity because they could have much of importance to say. Norman Brook never had to face retirement. He would not have liked it; he had had no time and no training for leisure. Schoolmasters not seldom retire from one school to another or take private pupils to whom they impart book learning acquired forty or fifty years before. University dons may retire from their fellowships but not from their research and not often from the university town which they have graced for most of their lives. Rebels are rebels for ever and women's work is never done.

The correspondence columns of *The Times* offer strong temptations to the retired man with a continuing confidence in his own opinions. The Editor of this invaluable forum must have a daily option of difficulties. Shall he reject the ex cathedra pronouncements of a retired Archbishop or the strategic certainties of an out-of-date Field Marshal? There is no room for both. He need not worry his tormented judgment too much.

If he rejects the Archbishop's letter, the Archbishop, nothing daunted, will send it direct to the unfortunate correspondent whose opinions he is so keen to castigate. If the Editor proves continuously unreceptive of the pearls of wisdom offered to him, there are other markets open to the retired man. There are countless clubs and societies only too anxious to listen at least once to the reminiscences of his important life, and schools, which seem unable to get away from the strange tribal proceedings of a Speech Day, will be glad to welcome his old eminence and provide him with a captive audience for his carefully pondered admonishments.

But in the end he will have to try to be content to sit in the sun, to concentrate his longings and his hopes upon that corner of earth, with its 'little patch of sky and little lot of stars', which above all others smiles for him. He will have to forget the puny fame which flickered on his path, the active influence he seemed to himself to exert over others, to turn his back upon dispute and arguments, to take no more delight in pomp and pretence. He must be passive now, the old and tranquil genius of his home, a mature presence in his garden of constant change and fresh renewal, the tried and faithful husband of his loving wife, the calm counsellor of all who love him. Then he may, like Plantin 400 years ago, await peacefully in his own home the welcome arrival of Death.

INDEX

UNIVERSITY LIBRARY
NOTTINGHAM